*A Remembrance*
*to the OES Libraries*

FROM

MRS. WILLIAM C. WEBER, JR.

DECEMBER, 1991

**OES**

**Oregon Episcopal School**

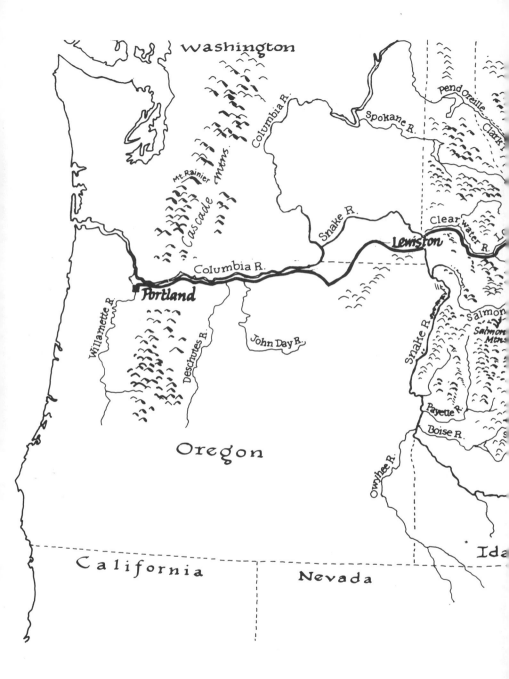

A journey from Oregon up the

Montana

Missouri R.

Musselshell R.

issoula

Lolo

Beaverhead R.

Madison R.

Lemhi R.

Yellowstone R.

Bozeman

Absarokee

Red Lodge

Powell

Big Horn R.

Bighorn Mts.

Yellowstone Park

Absaroka Range

Cody

Meteetse

Teton Ra.

Thermopolis

Victor

Swan Valley

Jackson

Dubois

Shoshone

Ft. Hall

Wind R.

Pocatello

ake R.

Wind River Ra.

Dayton

Utah

Wyoming

Lochsa Road (lŏck-săw) to Wyoming.

## Books by Kim R. Stafford

Prose

*Rendezvous: Stories, Songs, & Opinions
of the Idaho Country*
*Having Everything Right: Essays of Place*
*Entering the Grove*
*Lochsa Road: A Pilgrim in the West*

Poetry

*Braided Apart* (with William E. Stafford)
*A Gypsy's History of the World*
*The Granary*
*Places & Stories*

*Lochsa Road*

A Journey from Oregon up the Lochsa Road (Lŏck-sǎw) to Wyoming

A James R. Hepworth Book

# Lochsa Road

## A Pilgrim in the West

## Kim R. Stafford

Illustrations by Hannah Hinchman

Confluence Press

Thanks to the editors of *Northern Lights*,
where part of this book first appeared.


Publication of this book is made possible by grants
from the Idaho Commission on the Arts, a State
agency, and the National Endowment for the Arts
in Washington, D.C., a Federal agency.

ISBN: 0-917652-92-4 (cloth)
ISBN: 0-917652-93-2 (paper)

Library of Congress Card Number 91-71651

*Published by*

Confluence Press, Inc.
Lewis-Clark State College
8th Avenue & 6th Street
Lewiston, Idaho 83501-2698

*Distributed to the trade by*

National Book Network
4720-A Boston Way
Lanham, Maryland 20706

# Contents

# Lochsa Road

## A Pilgrim in the West

# Heart of the Monster

ONE MORNING IN APRIL when I was three, I announced I wanted to go jump into the daylight. But there are too many roads, I said. Where is the daylight, my parents asked. I pointed toward the east. About twenty miles, I said. I kept threatening to go, so they said goodby. Only my brother tried to dissuade me. He walked me to the corner, then went back. I crossed the creek, passed our landlord's house, followed a path toward the trees. Something awaited me. I had my boots on. Later, my father found me standing in front of the tavern in town. We talked for awhile, then he took me back. When I was bigger, we decided, I might go.

Since that day, I take that path when I have need. The daylight is the great hospitality of the world. Dawn calls, April calls, even fear and trouble call me out. I yield, venture, stumble. Maybe at the heart of it, the daylight is what the Paiute call the second night, the deeper one, just before dawn.

In Chaucer's time travelers took the road, vowing to visit shrines with holy names. Swarms of folk would ramble the road to Canterbury, for thumb-sized vials of miraculously diluted blood of the martyr Thomas; to Compostella in Spain for the cockle shell amulet of St. James; to Lourdes and Rome and Jerusalem for the healing of limb and heart and mind. Leaving the social suffocation of their villages in spring, wan travelers would hit the road with a staff and a prayer. *Thanne longen folk to goon on pilgrimages.* They became strangers, citizens of the world. That in itself can heal. These pilgrims sampled the hospitality of villages or scrounged from fields they passed. Their diet broadened and their hearts drummed. Charity, thievery, blessing, and curse all hastened them. The scrappiest vagabonds went clear to the ends of the world's roads and came back changed, or perished on the way. They chose it thus, to seek a healing place far from home. And I was of their company anon.

Certain places heal, places where the earth gives bounty. In my territory, too, the old ways include a kind of pilgrimage. The Paiute people of the American West, the Shoshone people, the Washoe, the Nez Perce bands, tribes of the Crow, Arapaho and Bannock wandered the mountains, the valleys, the sage benchlands, seeking out hidden springs, meadows fat with camas root, ravines stuffed with deer. Carrying willow basket bottles sealed with pitch, their children ran for water at dawn. Women set out with digging sticks for roots, and men with hemp nets for ducks and quail. And at certain places, they came up against the boundary of the sacred, found it by the old path of hunger, danger, intention, and surprise. In the brush hut at night, an old one told stories, chanting them softly while smoke went up through the smokehole toward the stars. In the stories, something happens to travelers. A pine tree beckons, a hawk's shadow crosses your path. Rain falls; the sky utters thunder. A tingling of fragrance rises from the earth to find you, an owl's soft cry, a star. In the stories, when winter eased its grip the people all set out, and they found food, and the stars found husbands, woman married bear, someone stole fire from the sun, and grieving coyote sought his woman in the distances of night.

When I was eleven, I found it hard to sit in school. Through the window, I could see the woods, just there, where the canyon sloped away, and in my mind I had a way to go. In my mind I would hurl a dictionary through the window, climb out through the jagged frame, and run for the daylight. A book might make the small door for me, the door to something deeper than my culture. I would seek that deeper thing.

Then, as I grew, I lost the path. I forgot about my daylight. When I was twenty, and in love, I took her to the forest, we married, and that would be everything. We spent our honeymoon in the wilderness, made camp at a place called Separation Creek. We set up house in the city, and bought a car. We set up a loom and a desk. We went to school and took odd jobs. We had a life, and I had a plan. For a decade, in my twenties, I joined my culture by earning wages, and fled my culture by reading. I would burrow into the oldest English books, stowing away with medieval writers for the journey. I waited by the sleepers with Beowulf, hit the road with the pilgrim Chaucer, scribbled old romance in Mallory's cell. I reeled through dreams with William Langland, and chanted confessions of love with John Gower. By the old magic of reading, I was in the castle chamber when Sir Gawain risked his life for a ribbon of green and a kiss. Sometimes I might leave my windowless room at the library to walk to the river, or find joy with my wife, but then I came back, for I chose to read myself into being. It was a choice studded with beauties, and fraught with monkish dangers. Books took me to the forest, to the wild of the past, to primitive tribal ways, the crags of poetry, the caverns of myth. I found scraps of delight boxed in books. At midnight I would be in my cell, stuffed with words but starving, filled with a longing I didn't understand.

Then, with a Ph.D. and its twin companion—a sense of exile from the actual world—I began to venture from our home. I was ripe with knowledge, and haunted by a vacancy that only wandering seemed to answer. I had schooling, but my soul was away without leave. I tried to call it back, not in my city, not at my desk, but somewhere outside all that. I tried to find places that might heal me. I went to Separation Creek alone, followed an abandoned trail beyond our camp. I slept on hillsides, followed rivers. I entered the trance of fast roads, parked to sleep, walked the night corridors of distant city streets, or followed a path by starlight into the wilderness. And I came to places. In the West, in the country that had chosen me, I found places that kept old habits from when the world was made. The place was a hidden spring, secret water at its mossy lip. Was a stream shouting and jostling stones. My breath came deeper in the din. I followed, and willows thickened at the confluence, where driftwood reached high after floods had whittled it white, had strewn it through the trees. A joining of rivers could mend my soul for a time, where one rainstorm's habitation slid its flank against another's, and my split lives fell hammered into one. The hawkish summit of a ridge could heal, a cave could take me into the earth. A desert cottonwood gave me shade from the killing sun.

We lived in the city, my wife and I. Good times came, like a storm of sunlight, and then they departed. When I could, I traveled to see how others lived. Distant jobs and places took me, and I went willingly. My journey could be Alaska, it could be New York, Texas, the mountains of Georgia. In our city, I dwelt with my wife, then with my wife and child, our car, then our cars, and our jobs. The story is long and strange. After seventeen years together, we had failed. She left me. I left her. We lived in one house. I would open a book, I would hold our child, with love in my hands. And my wife, she would bring sweet music from her wood flute, and warm colors from the loom. But there was no touch between us. It was all books and wool and sorrow. How could we live this way? I saw our lives teaching our daughter that man and woman don't touch each other. We didn't laugh, we didn't celebrate, some days we barely spoke. I lay awake nights, passing without a word or touch into the heart of grief. I believed my wife did the same, for in that house we turned away. First, it was a matter of talk dwindling to silence, of a hand withdrawn. Later the distances were made of miles and of years. It became a kind of killing. Rivers join, deepen. But we divided, we dwindled. We practiced a slow suicide, taking our lives a little at a time.

We were fools to let our love wither. Or maybe we were exactly the fools we had to be. I took the risks of the road, the easy ones. Sometimes I found a greater danger in safety at home. What was safe about sorrow? About sorrow, I can't tell it all. Ours was private and strange. Perhaps it is so for many. But about the healing—the healing has been mine, and I wish to tell its beginning.

I loved our daughter. She was six, and she told me, "Dad, did you know part of love is being brave?" Yes. Some desperate change might lead toward life, new lives, for each of us.

At the deepest times, I felt the pull of deserts. I felt the pilgrim road call me to healing places curve by curve, to valley, ridge line, peak. I was a professional of words, a teacher working at a college, but I felt the tug of stone silence. After a time at home, a binge of college work, I felt homesick for the road. At home, in the barn I had built out back, I would stay up all night working at my desk without a word. At my chair, with elbows propped left and right of a thick document, I often inhabited a stretch of night. And at the college, for days and for years, I practiced every scrivener's invention of endless labor: a swarm of detail protected me from the long view for a time. Then I had to go seek it.

When I was 38, my calling came with a two-week string of workshops in the open land: a week at the college in Powell, Wyoming, then a reading in Jackson, a meeting with students in Dayton, Idaho, a conference in Coeur d'Alene. On that circuit I could drive and ponder, walk the hills and get pitch on my hands, listen at the ridgeline, maybe start an answer. For Wyoming, I rose at 3:00 a.m. on a Saturday and crept to my college desk, for I had to finish a crush of minor tasks to earn the privilege of leaving town. I worked through that day silent and alone, blurred in the paper blizzard, and finally climbed into the car to go at 2:00 a.m. Sunday. It was April. I couldn't find my watch, or my Swiss army knife, or the notebook I always carry in my heart pocket to record conversation, idea, song scrap, dream. Let them go. I had my guitar in my old car, my sleeping bag, and a box of clothes.

East up the Columbia Gorge my car pierced the headlight tunnel of the road. I felt confusion for the wife I had left behind. Silent roommates, we had struck that bargain somehow without a word: to live together but separate and alone. My mouth began to shape a blues as I drove.

> I know I gave her sorrow,
> Yes, I know I gave her sorrow.
> It's the deepest thing I own.

> I'll gather my belongings,
> Take them on down the road,
> That's the deepest thing I know.

> I'll gather all my troubles,
> Won't leave behind my troubles,
> They're the deepest thing I own.

> I loved you with sorrow.
> I came through years with sorrow.
> It's the deepest thing I own.

Fatigue engraved those words into memory. My voice droned them deep, wind hushed past the car, and I followed the headlights' flared advance fringed with cottonwood leaves. With the window down so the cold wind might keep me wakeful, I felt the rush of the road, like being inside the river, throbbing upstream. My soul was naked now, and I felt the quick friction of my migration toward some smallest tributary of my being, rooted somewhere in the mountains far and lost and certain. Then it all blurred, and I slowed. One hour out, at 3:00 a.m., I stopped at the gravel edge of the road to sleep.

When I get that far gone, my whole body holds a heartbeat buzz. Fatigue yanks me down. I sprawled at the back of my station wagon, between guitar and box where I had spread my sleeping bag. But I was too shot to lift my feet and slide inside. Let the cold wake me, I thought. Safecrackers thin the skin of their fingertips with sandpaper to better feel the feather click of the knurled safedoor knob. Sleeplessness does that for all of me—and cold, and hunger. Even sorrow. Utter exhaustion gets me tuned for learning. A run of long haul trucks roared past, the car's chassis swayed, my mind stuttered, and I in my steel cradle slept.

Something jumped me—a maze, a rhythm of story, a dream. Waking, I just had strength to clutch it. In the ragtag journey of the dream, I traveled through a whirl of foggy places, met by stranger, squinting at the sun, threading a ravine, touching the sleeve of a woman. From that trance I sat up in a blur, but from the heart of the dream, I just had words for it, writ on the wall of my skull: *Life Tuition*.

Life tuition? This, by my sleep sense, was that portion of stamina one spent to learn. Nothing came free, and money couldn't buy this. Maps and plans failed to find it. Only a quick squandering got it. It was 3:15. My hand came down to slap my thigh, to wake me with a tingling. I crawled forward, propped myself at the wheel, and drove on east through the gloom. In the deepest darkness to the east, I knew there was dawn, like knowing by the look in a man's face he has a match in his pocket.

I had to be in Powell to teach a class at 1:00 p.m. Monday afternoon. If this was Sunday morning, 3:15, and I was one hour out from Portland, I figured a long straight run of thirty hours, with a break here and there to doze or ramble. My body obeyed something dense as the wish of an old fish, and I sped. At sunrise, I stopped to take on a speeding ticket at the Idaho border, dawdled to wake in Lewiston, walking cement sidewalks to shock and jostle my mind. And I was gone east up the Clearwater. By Sunday noon, I had made it to Kamiah.

Idaho, sometimes confused with Ohio and Iowa by distant travelers, is blessed with many shibboleths in its own odd names for village, prairie, river, and sacred place. The meadow where the Nez Perce people first met Lewis and Clark, and gave them food, is called Weippe (not 'wee-pea' but 'wee-ipe'). The village on the Clearwater is Kamiah (not 'kuh-my-yuh' but '*ka*-me-eye'). The tributary of the Clearwater that leads toward Lolo Pass is the Lochsa (not '*lotch*-sah' but '*lock*-saw'). Passing through Kamiah, on my way to the Lochsa, I pulled off the highway at the Heart of the Monster.

Maybe you know the story there.

Maybe you heard the story many times—how the Swallowing Monster inhaled all earth dwellers into his mouth, swallowing grizzly, rattler, muskrat, fox into his gut, until Coyote took five obsidian knives, and a fire kit, and got himself swallowed with the others. Coyote stepped along the dark and slime inside that rib tunnel. He breathed the stink and his feet kicked bones. He met some survivors, scrappy and peevish, kicked rattler in the face, blunted grizzly's nose. "Oh, you're fierce," he said to them, "but you haven't saved the people, for all your cunning and strength." Then Coyote kindled fire in the bonehouse, cut fat from the monster's heart to feed them all, and applied his first obsidian blade to the strings that held the heart in place, that big drum heart of the monster tethered pounding to the ribs inside. He cut and broke the blade, cut and splintered the blade five times. When his knives were gone he tore the last sinews with his fingers, the heart sprang free, and the monster erupted everyone away across the mountains where they would live. Coyote distributed fragments from the monster's body out beyond the horizon on all sides, and those fragments came to life as the neighboring tribes.

But then Fox said, "Did you give no thought for a people in *this* place?" Coyote washed his hands, and drops of the monster's blood fell in the dust, and there the Nez Perce people came into being, the real people, the *Ne-mee-poo* of the place. The heart itself fell here, the big stone heart inert in its meadow on the Clearwater, one riverbend east from Kamiah.

My government built a path for visitors, with blacktop and numbers on posts, but I'd lost all wish to follow. I struck out toward the meadow, circled the stone heart mound against the sun, kept it to my left.

The Indian people have a way of turning at the boundary

of a dance, or a sacred place. I have seen it at the Root Feast at Warm Springs, I have seen it at Young Joseph's grave. It is a way of making a hinge-footed door of the self, and stepping past what you used to be. I am still trying to learn it. That day I stumbled, turning at the meadow's edge, stepped toward the humped shadow the stone heart made. Inside the wood fence there, a garden of native plants bristled into the sunlight with greens, blues, and yellows. Flowers in Eden don't have names. I did not feel botanical, but hankered for blur and motion. A butterfly, the first I had seen that season, flickered beyond the fence. I stood at the edge. My gaze softened into the place: purple flowers clouded on a stem, and the yellow butterfly folding light and shadow where it flashed.

To the south, in a stand of locust trees where the path circled, I came upon a post with Coyote etched in plastic at the top, and a small sign said I might push a button to hear the story there. The locust trees behind me rattled empty. It was April, off-season, and everything seemed shut down. I stood by the post and pushed the button anyway. There was a beat of silence, I took a breath, then a meadowlark called from somewhere by the river, beyond the mullein stalks silver with light, and blackbirds chanted from the reeds that rustled, and I could hear wind coming upriver through cottonwoods, flipping the young leaves against each other, and then a pair of ducks wheeling where the river turns, and children laughing in the Lewis and Clark Trailer Court across the highway.

The story on the tape was dead for winter, and the world had begun to tell. I began to feel released from something. When a bud case splits, the leaves come full. Like meadowlark, like laughter, my life might be part of the telling.

On the road again, I reached back for that song of meadowlark, the song that flows like cold water from the earth. Whenever sleep reached for me, and my head jerked and waggled at the wheel, I stopped to wash my face in the river, to shatter chill water over my head, to slap my fist against a stone, shout, dance on the sand. As I climbed higher up that road, as I followed the Clearwater to the steeper run of the Lochsa, the seasons went backward, and I moved from cottonwood's first thin leaves, to an ice rim along the river, from the wakening meadow of Kamiah to the snowy trance of the firs higher up.

This was my road, my daylight. No book had it, or they all did, but they were not mine. I had been their passenger. Now I took the reins. Maybe Chaucer was of my company now, Chaucer and the Indians, and we had slipped away east out the school window. We were crowding along the road, and I was alone there, and driving. Somewhere on that road, a sign told how Lewis and Clark came west this way in the winter of 1805, stumbling out of the pines to meet the friendly Nez Perce, to eat, to trade for horses, to open the country for their president. Then I remembered how in July of 1878, the Nez Perce fled east over the Bitterroot Mountains here, chased by the army from their land along this same way. By my daylight, I traveled one of the grooves of change.

The river turned and the road obeyed. And I obeyed. Time got bigger. At my office in Portland, when I was sealed to my yellow swivel chair at midnight, I had been in such a trance of fatigue I had scribbled "budge," having no time to spell out "budget." Now, I drove a long way, and the sun moved hardly at all, daylight held, flickering through cedar over my shoulder, glancing wherever water shimmered. The sun stared, the river flashed and turned, and I drifted east in a white car that seemed to know the road that led toward Lolo summit.

# Where Everything Changes

WHEN MY HEAD SNAPPED BACK from a doze, I pulled off the road to the salt lick all creatures favored. I followed the trail awhile, then punched off it to ramble the cedar grove where logs lay jumbled and sulfur steam rose from the earth, the black earth elk licked for salt. Their tongues had hollowed holes in the dirt, so deeply they craved it: a hoofprint, another hoofprint splayed in mud, and then the wet cleft where the tongue reached down for savor. I felt the prickle of something lusty about the place, the air rank, and spindles of hair clinging to logs the elk had rubbed. My body worked the aisles of the log tangle, walking a cedar trunk, hopping to a boulder, peering inside a hollow snag.

Far uphill from the trail, I sat on a log to rest, and slipped into a trance. It wasn't sleep, exactly, but a blurred slide of memory flooding like a river. Cedar logs radiated from me, silver and gray, and I could hear the river talking. Somewhere in the stones of its bed, behind my half shut eyes, below the stars of my native city, before American history bristled across this continent like thistle in a camas prairie, the river spoke to me there. It spoke thirst and trouble, blues and laughter, moss and pitch. It fed me a whisper of skin thrill and eye dazzle, it swirled in place and centered me. If a place could unravel itself with stories, if I could read their languages, I might carry a healing from it.

When I opened my eyes, I studied the exact fallen architecture of the cedars. Some stood, some leaned on a wood shoulder, some lay side by side. My gaze walked the whole circumference of that place, the green trees and silver snags, hoof-trampled mud, my shoes, my folded hands. By my hip, I spotted a slip of paper wedged in a crack of the cedar log I sat on. Between my fingers it had that worn silk feel of a note folded many times, unfolded, then hidden in itself again. On one side in faded blue print it said, "Thank You." On the other it said, "Guest Check," and writ neat there was a woman's name, Tracy, and a phone number, Missoula prefix.

My mind ran through stories: Maybe Tracy wanders the wilderness, leaving her number where her kind of man might find it. Or maybe her mother wanders the wilderness, leaving her daughter's number where a man might find it. Or maybe a drifter, someone like me, met Tracy, took her number, but had a sense at the salt lick his pack was too heavy by just the feather weight of her name, and he wedged it in the cedar crack for another. I glanced around at the cedars, dark, dying, green. My heart pounded, my breath came short. I felt a chill graze my cheek. The salt and the cedars had me. I inhabited a place of love and no love, where the salty kiss we give each other gives way to solitude, and solitude longs to be dissolved with a kiss again. The muscle of the tongue, of the heart works this boundary. I work this boundary, living what I see. I savor these customs at the margin of the wilderness—these habits of longing, of wishes half revealed. Where elk licked the earth I felt the pang.

Of the possible stories that place told, I liked best the woman as actor in her own life, companion to whim. She knew it's a danger to live an opening life, a life that faces the stranger. But she knew it is death to live shut. As she traveled, she yielded, nudged by the raw intensity of the natural world to make an act at once dangerous and necessary. She stood at the edge where transformation begins, left her number there.

The greatest sin against your own life is to know what you want, and not to act.

A few miles on up the Lochsa road, I noticed a tick on my knee, seeking along in its eight-leg way for a place to feed. Where I smelled elk, I should have known the brush would be lousy with ticks. From the car on the road shoulder, I bounded upslope through deep snow crusted over, breaking through and floundering, scrambling up an icy log until I was out of sight in the trees. In that shaded room of forest, I shed my clothes, hanging coat, shirt, shoes, pants, shorts, and socks on branches until I stood naked on the snow. Time got bigger again. I felt empty and clean, cold, nameless. I brushed my body, shook out my clothes, fingered my hair for ticks. Found seven. Flicked them away. Shivered awhile.

It should have been evening. But the sun stayed high, white through haze. The snow hill I stood on held an internal icy glow, where my feet melted tracks in the crust. Wind fed me cedar, jaysong, riversound, pine. Wind suckled at my body for warmth. I shifted my feet. I seemed to be perched on one of those pinnacles of change I kept coming to, kept inhabiting for a moment before leaning forward and going on. The cold helped me exhale everything. My bones felt tattered by fatigue. I tried to stand like a trunk, but I shook like a twig.

As I lifted my coat from a cedar limb, my notebook fell from the pocket where it didn't belong, fell open on the snow. I dressed and shivered down to the car, and there, when I opened the door, under the seat I saw the gleam of my watch where it had slipped from my pocket. On a hunch, I lifted a pair of gloves from the floor on the passenger side. There was my lost redhandled knife. I arranged notebook, watch, and knife on the seat beside me, drove on steady up the Lochsa rumbling white down the boulder gorge of its making.

Time got slow. Life got big. I earned my tools back by standing in the snow to shiver empty.

The Lochsa travels by the impulse of steep, young rivers,

turning with a water shout at boulders, at logs, smashing through patches of forest that have slid into the current. The river itself marks the boundary of the Selway Bitterroot Wilderness. Here and there a footbridge crosses from common forest to the territory we leave alone, from highway to trail, from calendar to the eternity of pitch, green leaf, lightning. Once, sliding toward sleep, I parked and crossed over. The river was high, I turned at the center, and stood a moment at the boundary of shadow the ridge cast down.

Down there in the water, I could glimpse the blue hump of a boulder, as the roil of reflection cleared a moment, and then the swaying shadow of a fish on the sand, then the fish itself hovering just where it best fit the current. I saw deep into the Lochsa's mind where the fish aimed east. The river was not a place but a way of happening.

Then the surface quivered again, reflection closed my gaze, and I watched the surface in its busy work, its muscle of ripple and slap. I ran for the car, the narrow suspension bridge swayed, and I drove the boundary east.

The top of Lolo Pass is a place where everything changes. Do you know these places in your life, these risky pinnacles? I find I must honor them. I find every road haunted by these turnings, these threshholds—every river, every path, every friendship. Every river climbs from its turmoil at the eddy and goes on, the kinks in the current stretching and opening, flaring out. The road narrows at the summit, and threads the cliffs. A deer path leaves the pines, crosses an uneasy trance of scree. And the turnings of friendship deepen, ricochet, web, until there comes the steady gaze by candlelight. It's a long time coming, until it seems like never. You feel the pull, without knowing the destination. You go down into sorrow, sometimes, being that close, but not finding a way out, not finding a connection. When these changes tug me to a new place, I enter the monster of myself, cut at the heart, and emerge as best I can. From the blood, sometimes, comes new life.

If you drive the same road many times, they all become one. Time, distance, and speed are small, and the place is big.

16

Memory climbs onto this time now, and rides. Once before, at Lolo Summit, I met a pillar of fire, a soundless burning at dusk that consumed nothing but time. I stood among the trees to watch it, a soft tornado the color of sunset, climbing like the twist of an old pine. One voice in me said I might have called the district ranger crew at Powell. This was their territory, their jurisdiction, but not their dimension. The fire hovered above the trees in a ravine, rooted to nothing, flickering in a spiral like wind tethered in place, its naked writhe. It had no smell, no smoke, only a whisper of sound. It whispered, and I closed my mouth. Then I felt it burning part of me, sipping deep where change takes root.

This time, just over the summit, I came upon the freshly burned hulk of a car smashed against the bank at the end of a long set of skid marks. The windshield was shattered, and the rim of the hood seared. When I leaped from my car this time I smelled the fire but heard nothing. No one was inside. On the driver's seat lay the clenched chrome knuckles of the seatbelt, and a comb.

I looked around at the darkening trees. No one. The driver must have hitchhiked with a stranger, a pilgrim.

I gathered into my mind that pillar of fire, the traveler's burnt car, my tattered life, and the days running. I took this warning and drove carefully down into Montana, a new time zone, darker, slow at the evening deer hour, through the town of Lolo, north to Missoula, onto the interstate, then cruising east at full dark. My journey had slid me into a deep trance. I would take a two hour run, thundering along among the long haul convoys of truck and tourist. We would climb a tough slope together, then scatter down the far side, weaving past each other, then schooling into a pack at the next steep grade. And then the headlight dance would blur for me, and I would pull off to crawl into the back of the car for a taste of sleep, a small dream, and then shout awake, "Okay!"

When the night got cold, I would jog around the car four times under the stars to sharpen my mind. Driving, I would chew gum till my jaws ached, then chew the ache numb, slap my thigh. I would open the window to buffet my face with wind, and shout songs, squeaking in my reach to harmonize with the engine's drone. I would bite my tongue for the kernel of pain, turn on radio static full blast just for the thrill, suckle bitter coffee from styrofoam. This was not the first time I had risked my life to teach a class. But some ache battered me. I drove, but I was driven.

And then west of Bozeman, parked in gravel just beyond the reflective medallions of the road, I dreamed a happy woman was trying to kindle laughter from a formal man. She was blond; he was Japanese. Her festive garments billowed loose; his black suit clung snug. He was small, and held still; she was tall, and danced around him, tugging on his sleeve, chattering, whispering, beginning a sentence with words and ending with laughter.

A truck's buffeting woke me. I lunged for the wheel, thinking I dozed there, but my hands closed on nothing. My body stirred, like a marionette in a tangle of string. I crawled forward to the wheel, and drove. Of course, in the dream both man and woman were me, the man driving alone toward my work, while the woman dwelt mute in my life, her fine hilarity of pleasure lost somewhere, her genius for laughter numbed by loneliness. South of Absarokee, I flickered past a small house with a wood sign at the mailbox: the names Lon and Lou with a heart whittled between them. Something in me sought that link—behind travel and residence the serious happiness that woman and man can make. How could this begin with me, the faithful husband estranged, apart, the one who would not call a woman in Missoula, but could not love his wife at home? The long act of not loving numbs. Solitude had become a tightrope I could almost manage. The highway curved through barren hills, and I obeyed it.

Somewhere in the haze of that morning I remember glimpsing a coyote, down in a draw I saw for one second as I flashed past at sixty-five. She crouched, dun colored like the grass, working at the second strand on a new stretch of sheep fence. She was wrenching that strand aside to leave a slot at the fence corner. Her path had been interrupted. She restored it. I was a blur, she was poised, and we shared a glance.

Her eyes said, "I will run, if you make me, but I own this life. I travel nights, and I don't mind fences so long as I know the places I can slip through."

Then I was gone, and she did her work with the wire, and I did mine. Maybe she had spoken it all with that look. Maybe my dreams said everything I might need. Maybe the tick urged parables on me that I shivered from. In some configuration of the landscape lay the tools for understanding my heart's work. If I paid attention, maybe another life would grow from this withering. Driving, I dreamed. Sleepless, I fed. My heart pumped me forward through the miles. To my bruised mind, the landscape had become bare geology. Somewhere, I might pick up the trace.

East and south from Red Lodge, I rolled into Powell, Wyoming, found the college, and drifted into the lobby of the Humanities Building just as the sweep second hand of the wall clock swung up toward 1:00 p.m. My host was turning away to cancel my first class when I called his name.

"Rob? I'm Kim. I'm here." He looked me up and down, and conducted me to a room that shimmered fluorescent, and sixteen faces swung toward me. For this task I risked my life curve by curve? My reputed wisdom was a blur, but stories came easy, songs tumbling from my mouth, poems unraveling smoothly from my recitation mind.

My motel that night was a species of paradise simply because it contained a horizontal place to lay my body down.

# White Stone Knife on polecat Bench

AFTER A FEW DAYS IN POWELL, I was hunched over coffee at the Skyline Cafe with the early morning shift, when a thin old gentleman beside me offered this commentary:

> Son, you can go down to the variety story and get yourself a little bitty alligator no bigger than a lead pencil and feed it bits of hamburger every day for a hundred years and it won't grow at all, but you start giving it whole hamburger patties on a plate and it will turn into a god-damned monster overnight, and that's just what happened to our federal government!

He sipped his coffee, smacked his lips, satisfied. I nodded. I felt ready to agree. But then I thought about me. What kind of monster was I? What kind of feeding did I need? My body held a big order of pancakes, but my spirit wilted yet, a spindly child. My friend Rob had told me where: I needed a ramble up on Polecat Bench, north of town, to restore my soul.

I took the straight road north that turns west when it hits the slope. It was early spring, and they had fires everywhere, burning out the Frannie Canal and its lateral ditches before the irrigation flood came through. I got up on top, turned off on a side road, bounced along awhile, dust prickling my nose, the good glare of morning putting a halo around every bug on the windshield. At first glance, things look pretty bleak up there on top. My spirit feeds on quiet things. The real place doesn't come with postcards or a map, just the fine details accumulating for miles, and for years, and then the big story comes up on you from behind. The landscape springs upon you all at once, at the moment you realize you have been inviting it to stalk you for years.

Where the south rim of the bench began to break up into a series of canyons and bald stone knobs, I left the car and went down along a slot that started in sage and simplified into bare clay, a light gray green, crumbled small. Scuffling along, I felt easy. When I was young, I hunted. Later, I carried a camera. But lately, I just try to go be there. Be still. Listen.

I was listening my way across a sterile hill of clay when I bent to pick up the white stone knife, about as long as my hand, with little rose spots on it. There was nothing else around, no plant, no creature, no sign that hillside had been different for a good long time. Maybe the stone knife fell from the rabbit fur sheath at the belt of someone traveling like me, simply to cross the hill, to thread through the breaks, up sandstone canyons, startling an owl as I had, singing to deer as I had, going on somewhere through this country.

A little bird sang, I couldn't tell where. Wind had a way of bringing filaments of sound from far off. I turned the knife over in my hand. It still held the chill of night. A few deft nicks on the working edge would have made it keen again. I slipped it back into its sheath in the earth, and went on.

Deep in a ravine, it gave me joy to find a pool of gray water where the flash flood from our last rain had slipped away, leaving the puddle socketed in mud. In the sand I saw tracks of deer, coyote, rabbit, sage hen, mouse—all the creatures stepping up lightly to taste something gray and wet. Without it this place would be mere geology, only light and wind and stone. I could feel a river of air flowing down the ravine. The pool fed its village of owl, deer, coyote, butterfly, pine, moss, and these bundles of purple flowers just now at their prime.

Reaching the high ground again, I came to a bare knob of sandstone, ten feet high. In the dust at my feet lay fourteen flakes of flat black stone where they had been split off the spall some years or centuries ago. They lay together still, just where someone had stopped to work on the sunny side of the knob on a winter afternoon deep in the old time. That worker took the shaped tool, left the splintered flakes. Sun hammered them softly now. They clicked together in my hand when I picked them up. Then I set them down and went on.

The sun had climbed, and I shunned the open slopes for the shaded slots of broken ground. I followed water's path, treading sand where it swirled along, brushing low branches aside, hopping off a lip of stone into a pool of shadow. The Skyline Cafe's pancakes had worn off, but something else took hold. I tasted dust, inhaled a pine snag's pitch at a recent lightning strike. The place was feeding me sensations of color and grit. Birdsong came to me in little tufts, like five-needle pine. I had left the map in my car. I carried the kind with footprints on it, with a pinch of sand between my teeth.

In the shade of a twisted pine, with my hand where wind had polished its bare shoulder, I felt the longing of this place, how it spoke through flint chip and water pool of a possible and very different way to live with exactly the same resources of woman and man, childhood and age, rain and stars, night, fire, chlorophyll, cold, pine, stone, and desire. History gives us a set of possibilities. Imagination gives us a set. I had put the stone knife down, but its ragged shape had left a pleasure in my hand. To leave the car, to abandon food for a day, to be led across broken country by the flicker of sunlight and beckoning shade—these educate. For I am an idiot with a Ph.D. In the desert, I know this. It is not that we would ever go back. But the old ways give permission to range wide in mind, to think crazier than strict logic, to lean forward in our search for new traditions. History is primarily a tool for the imagination, and imagination can start new habits for survival.

I looked down the canyon's slot at the burning ditches of my people. We have learned to clear the land's grooves with fire, and then to invite water to come along. Our ways are primitive. We may be wrong to live thus. We survive in our time, and we learn in little ways to cast our minds outward, to receive the land and its visions. We won't be home until we listen low to the earth.

Up on the bench a hammerhead oil pump pivoted endlessly with a moan, sucking oil from deep stone strata. A sign warned me there: "This property patrolled by armed private security personnel to guard against theft. Trespass at your own risk. Danger." I felt I was being warned about a wild animal, that the oil company could not be expected to be responsible for the actions of its guard. I trespassed at my own risk, walking toward the rig. Sometimes a gust of wind made me turn, raising the hackles on my neck. But I finally came to the moving shadow of the rig, the big head that rose and swung down, swung up, swung down. The gleaming steel of the shaft, where it slid into the pipe in the earth, drew my eye to a name painted white on the rig's face: "Wendi S." The letters were roughly made, just where the iron head swelled, and the drill pivoted as it swung. And I suddenly felt the longing of the place. I felt how being long without love made love act odd things. Maybe the workers named each pump for a woman, saying, "Let's go see Wendi, see how she's doing." Or maybe the armed private security guard, with his gun and his lonely beat, painted this woman's name.

I saw a silver glint high against the blue, a jet drifting east, spinning out a soft white trail behind it. I knew a meal of oil sent it high; the pump beside me launched it. Bending my neck to follow, I felt like a passenger and a victim. We can all be part of the world's vulnerability, all citizens of fear without trying at all. But to be part of the world's healing, a citizen of change, takes choice. I wanted to touch this land, brag about it, sweeten the souls of my people with a fragrance underfoot. The right pleasure will save us. Sensation will bring us home. We all might walk and listen here. I will achieve loyalty to this earth, my country, where the stripes are seasons and the stars are stars.

The pump swung up and down. The jet drifted east. I drove here. The pump brought me to this place, for my car, too, suckled the refinements of oil. I had much to learn.

My eyes were open, but I opened them again. A barren place bristles with detail. The sun revels in the textured skin of every stone, every pebble's knuckle, every wrinkle of dust printed by wind. At the edge of my shadow an ant gleamed against the white dust. Spirit, having no place to hide, walked abroad and small in the sunlight. I walked across the wide land, where wind made the grasses bend and quiver. I pulled out the beaded pouch I wore on a string under my shirt, opened its tiny mouth, and slid a flake of red flint inside, a fleck the people had left, to work in the pouch with chokecherry seed from the root feast, with a tip of pine needle from the mountain top, and a wraith of moss from the grove. I staggered the scree slope of a canyon off the bench, savored the way last light held the stone cliffs, found where a hawk had died, where the wind sent its feathers one by one away from the white bones of rib and wing. Some old sorrow came welling up in me, a custom of my heart at evening. When I began to have trouble seeing my footing, I climbed back up to the bench, set out west across it in the failing light.

On the flat blanket of the land, just after sundown, grass twitched, wind flung small birds past the rim and down into their canyons to rest, and evening settled over the bench. At the close of light, I came upon the tipi ring of stone. Maybe twelve feet across, with a shallow fire pit at the center where bunchgrass hunched, the stone ring spoke something. It would be foolish not to try to tell truth about this. I sat down outside, listened at the edge. I felt a density in the air where the old ones lived. I combed the grass with my fingers.

Down there, beyond the rim, in the lit grid of Powell, at the Homestead Museum I had seen my own people's ways of knowing this place. I had seen "a cleaning brush used by Ursula Kepler's mother for dusting steam radiators...made of hair from buffalo tails which is replacable when worn." I had seen the Shoshone Rock Club's Bicentennial "Our Heritage" diorama, with its arrowhead, rattlesnake rattle, fossil snail, and toy oil derrick. With the club, I saw all culture by the tapered glimpse of history. I had seen the photo of Mrs. Glen Mangus in her home, a converted barrack moved from the Japanese Relocation Center at Heart Mountain, 1947. I had read that Polecat Bench is one of the only places in the world "where the early Cenozoic diversification of mammalian life is recorded through such a long sequence of continuous sediments representing virtually continuous deposition."

Down there at the throbbing weekend heart of Powell, a sign on the corner notifies customers: "Likker Store. Discount likker. If you can buy your booze cheaper let us know." Cars circle the block, cars with names like Fiero and Fiesta, intent on making noise. I remembered the din of the tavern, where my head felt like a gunnybag of ice when someone swung the sledge to shatter it.

But here, up here by the plain ring of stone, wind rushed the grass, and I shivered. Up here, I clung to the land. The culture sent my kind to walk the boundary, a citizen who can't quite fit. I thought of things more distant and more intimate. I remembered the stone house they showed me in Laramie, built by the local eccentric son: crisp and solid hewn stone walls with no door and no roof. He felt closer to the sky, he said, than to his family or his neighbors. I remembered what the English a thousand years ago called the stone remnants of Roman occupation, *eald enta geweorc*, 'the old work of giants.' Shattered walls and single stone columns spoke then of that frightening but compelling heroic past. They saw in ruins not just the historic fact but the continuing possibility of a more coherent life.

At the tipi ring of stone, I stepped inside. The bunchgrass in the firepit flickered and twitched, and I sat by it. When the sky had fully darkened, stars came one by one, and then the multitude. Wind came cold and I was cold, but something held me there to sleep, to shiver and breathe deep, to wake and turn, over and over, to listen to the rawhide hand of the wind. I felt a kind of cold I could not shake from me. Wind tried to snatch my jacket away. Darkness had many colors, because it was all I had. I saw them, felt them chill and bite. Grass whistled against my head. Stars wheeled.

Maybe a rock felt like I felt, or a bone. My face was a mask the place wore, looking up to the stars. They circled, and I lay in a heap. In the morning, after starlight waned, I stood and turned four ways. The sky stood tall: rain falling in gray banners to the north, a flat blue vista to the west, a rolling stampede of fat clouds south, and white light through a dark cloud slit to the east. Each direction held a blessing and a storm for me. I would travel them all.

By 8:00 a.m. I was back to the car, back down that long straight road to Powell, back at the Skyline Cafe for breakfast. As I teetered on my counter stool to ponder the menu, the waitress gave the ticket wheel a whirl and called through the slot, "Al, I got an order, please. This lady wants two eggs poached well, and her bacon burnt. And you can't burn it too much or she can't eat it, and you can't not burn it enough or she won't." As I wrapped my cold hands around a cup of coffee, I remembered the place on Polecat Bench where the old ones had slaughtered buffalo, I guessed, where amid the dust and purple flowers the ground lay thick with flint hatchets and knives, where the people had taken their tools for a day's life direct from the ground, and then set those tools down and gone on somewhere. They went on, and I went on. I put the white stone knife back into its sheath of clay. I put my porcelin cup down on the yellow formica counter. I put my life into the hands of the earth.

# Climbing
# Heart Mountain

HIGH SUN MADE THE DUST STAND WHITE when wind spun it.
I stood at the bare plowed field that had been the Heart
Mountain Japanese Relocation Camp during World War II.
The straight dusty furrows of the place recalled a sentence
from history, as I had read that history in the Homestead
Museum in Powell: "From 1909, when the Powell area's
valuation was zero dollars, to 1980 when the valuation is now
$168,499,492., Powell has grown into a community of
progress." Something about that last $2 touched me: a child's
fortune listed in the aggregate. Here, where the city of Heart
Mountain had stood for a few years of the war, I looked at zero
now, the field, the chimney tower, a shed, the concrete abut-
ments where those frame barracks had perched in rows upon
rows. A ruin yearns. A tumbleweed jerked toward me, then
caught on barbed wire.

By the highway, the American Legion had erected a sign
telling the history of the camp, how "eleven thousand people
of Japanese ancestry from the three west-coast states were
loosely confined by the United States government in the
center for about three years." Wind hit the side of my face,

and I felt buffeted by facts: "First rate schooling was provided for the children of the evacuees through the high school grades." The sign was rooted in gravel, where cars might turn aside for a moment to learn the story, then drive on. I crossed the railroad tracks, leaving the highway, and read the more remote sign erected by the citizens of the camp itself, bleak and alone like a Zen stone garden: "Although surrounded by barbed wire and armed guards, the internees kept the camp functioning as a small city." The wind had torn away the names of camp boys who fought in Italy. How could I tell truth? On those two signs, my people talked to each other in my head. We left word on the land. The armed guards were gone, and most of the barbed wire was down, but I felt arrested, loosely confined, taught by the high sun on the place. Stories burned in the dust.

I remembered coming upon barrack buildings from the camp scattered one by one over the valley, where they had been uprooted and moved at the war's end. The internees had scattered to find homes in their country again, America. And the barracks of the camp had been trucked to farms and turned to garages, machine sheds, chickenhouses. But they were always recognizable by their dimensions, their minimal regularity. This field had held the third largest city in Wyoming. Out in the center of it now, the whirlwind spun.

By the brick spire I picked up a stone, hot from the sun, smooth where it fit my palm. I had to pass it hand to hand as it burned. It reminded my hand of the kind of stone they call a mano, a grinding stone the first people used to powder the seeds of desert grass. But this spoke of the camp. In the heated shimmer, I saw it slap laundry and spit water on the ribbed tin board over a tub. I pulled a shriek of tin aside and entered a long shed, where the hard light of the sun softened through smudged windows.

Cobwebs hung down in gauze, glass glittered, and an oildrum stove squatted on the concrete floor. By the stove in a heap lay hundreds of pegs, square at one end and round at the other, whiskered rough-cut wood. I studied one with my hands and recognized the stub leg of a barrack bunk, whittled round at the foot from two-by-two pine. And suddenly I saw the camp coming down, the people gone, the rows of barracks pried up, yanked onto trucks, rumbling away one by one under powdered columns of snow, and someone taking refuge here by the stove, burning the bunks, cursing the wind, holding a hand toward the flame, slamming the stove door shut.

Wind ruffled the tin roof now. Then it twitched with a ping in the heat.

With my Wyoming map and a wish, I drove in the general direction of Heart Mountain itself, that block of stone on the horizon to the west, blue in the smoky haze of ditch fires. I read its mark on the landscape, and obeyed its beckoning. The mountain made me tilt my head as I approached, an abrupt and lonesome peak. The geologists, I was told, are puzzled by it. It seems this mountain block of stone comes from sixty miles away, and lies upside down. Did it fly, spit and flipped by vulcanism to land with the old rock on top and the younger below? Did some glacial shoulder nudge it here, dozing south for centuries? No one seems to know.

I wanted to climb to the oldest stone, to put my hand on it. Its blue shape shimmered, distant. Out on the flats, I was lost on a maze of dusty roads, roving the square promises of fence line, ditch line, twin-rutted track. My map whipped in the wind where I stood by the car. When I slapped the map flat on the hot hood, I followed a road toward the mountain with my finger, but I had lost faith I might be on it.

Way off west stood a cowboy by the ditch, his head tilted to watch the water go by, his horse tethered to a fencepost. I followed the road to him, trying to ride the high ridge between ruts with my right wheels, and keep the left wheels on the shoulder. He watched my car roll and weave along the road, then turned back toward the water. I brought dust with me, and it swirled around him.

"Howdy," I said, standing by the car, "my name's Kim Stafford, I'm from Oregon, and I think I'm lost." He touched his hat. We stood awhile without a word. I could see the brown water gathering tumbleweeds into great rafts in the ditch at his feet.

"Bob Woodruff," he said. "Had to rest my horse." I stood beside him, my map crackling in the wind. The ditch ran full at our feet. A ribbon of foam trailed from where the tumbleweeds had jammed together. His horse shifted feet, dipped its head.

"So you're just out driving?" he said.

"Looking around," I said. "I went up Polecat Bench. Nice quiet country. Now I'm trying to walk up onto Heart Mountain. Can you tell me how to get to the foot of it?"

"Yeah," he said, "I can tell you." And his hand reached out, his finger following a branch of the road I'd been on, up to the ridge line, and beyond. "Get there, and stay on the high road," he said. "You can go down off north to a barn on the side, if you want to see it, and that road reconnects farther along. Or you can stay on top. You'll get to a spring, and that's a good place to leave your car. Got enough lime in it to give you flavor. Kind of curdle your soap but it tastes alright. That's all deeded land, and if you take care of it they'll let you in there. Just remember to close any gates you find closed, or leave them open if they're open."

He turned to the water again. The tumbleweed jam had loosened, and the whole mass rolled and slowly spun away.

"How did that Heart Mountain get named?" I said, shielding my eyes with the map.

"The name?" he said. "Doesn't seem like anybody knows." He looked toward the west, then down to his feet. "It's had that name for well over a hundred years," he said, "but as far as it being named after someone named Heart, nobody knows.

"Had a Navaho fellow working with me," he said, "running sheep one time. You get him off by himself and he's in the right mood, he'll tell you a little bit. They get together, they just talk Navaho and you can't tell what's going on. Anyway, he told me it's a sacred mountain. Said they had one like it down in his country. Didn't say much more."

He held his hand out. "But you see that ridge over there toward Sunlight Basin?" He raised his finger toward it."Yeah," he said, "the farthest, the blue one. My dad told how the army sat right here on this slope where we're standing, watching the Nez Perce come over that ridge. Watched through field glasses, watched them go down out of sight in the canyon, and waited. Thought they'd surely come on along the easiest way, straight on across. Then the army could engage the Indians out in this open country. But it turned out the Nez Perce got out of sight, they went on down—no one's quite sure which way they went." He brought his arm down, and closed his mouth in a kind of puzzled satisfaction.

The water in the ditch was rolling, after a winter of dry weather, and he kept talking, after his long ride alone. "Then," he said, "there's what they call Dead Indian Hill up at Sunlight. Some of the history books say that was Chief Joseph's warriors were the dead Indians. But what really happened was there was another time a little bunch of army guys camped down here by the cemetery, and they saw some Indians off on the horizon, so they left their camp and went after them, kind of grab them and get them back on the reservation. They used to like to do that. Well, there was one guy with them, they didn't know if his name was La Roque, and he was a French-Canadian fur trapper, or maybe his name was Little Rock and he was an Indian. He was with the army party as a scout. They all got to shooting and he got killed, and they buried him quick and went on after the Indians. They found one who'd made it as far as dead Indian hill, and died there, so they named it."

I looked away toward the mountain, a smudge of shadow under a gray sky. It acted like a relative who had turned up after years of traveling. "And Heart Mountain?" I said.

"You follow this road," he said, "and slip downhill off the main track to the north, you'll find a cabin up there by the sheep camp. They moved it a ways up the hill from where it sat, but it's original equipment. Probably built in '78, '80."

"Oh, it isn't that old?" I said. Mr. Woodruff looked at me.

His eyes danced and laughed like water glittering in place.

"Oh," I said, "you mean 1878."

"Yeah," he said, "a century." And then he went on, by the etiquette of the west, to humble himself, now that I had stumbled in my ignorance.

"I'm just going along today," he said, "putting in staples where barbwire fell off the posts. We'll come tomorrow with the truck to drive a few new posts so we can run the cattle."

A car passed us on the road, going fast and raising dust. Mr. Woodruff read the license plate, said, "Huh, 411, don't know them." He turned to me, without any particular expression, but the moment held a very quiet respect. He didn't know 411, but he'd remember OREGON DFD 448.

He touched his hat, and turned to his horse. My car was hot. I sat inside while he reined his horse around and followed the ditch away through the sage. And then I drove.

I drove the path of roads and gates and ridges where he sent me, turning off along the dirt track to seek the cabin, the barn, the sheep camp of his stories. At a cleft in the ridge, a few poplars rose up, and I walked down to them. The cabin was all the work of an ax, a deft century ago, with the palm-sized strokes of a sharp blade showing weathered and clean on the walls' tall corners, on the rafter ends, the door frame, the window sill. Sod covered the roof, a few parched grasses in the rain-channeled dust. A panel of sunlight entered the doorway and lay flat on the dirt floor. A small stove and an iron double bed almost filled the interior. For a moment, I was taken by whatever woman might have lived there with me a century before. My mind burrowed like a chigger through time, digging for the taste of life. Maybe there were curtains then, the soft light of a lamp. And down the slope of thistle and chin-high grass, I found the long palace of the sheep barn just beginning to sag, crowning high as a hill at the central ridge and easing toward earth at the eaves.

Inside, it was a long cool shimmer down the aisle of dust, of gates polished by sure hand and frightened fleece, of the workbench glazed with oil, of the sixteen numbered posts of the shearing stations raising their juniper columns at the nave. The walls showed slims of sunlight, and the whole room weathered a century's glimpse of sky. At the barn's southwest corner, just above the stock gate that opened into the coral, I saw the ceiling had been decorated. Light reflected up from the white dust outside, and on the tin roof I read the names of the shepherds, where they must have painted them at a break in the work, or at the season's end:

Len Lueck, 1938

Bob Simpson '29

Chuck 1918

WMC 1926

LDW CDW 1926 + 1929

RKW

14 Jack

And among the names I saw the designs of longing and companionship: a woman's face, her hair, eyes, and mouth stroked onto the tin with paint the color of tar. Her eyes held a steady gaze, and the curls around her face shaped her like a full moon, tilted to see me. Her eyebrows arched. Her mouth smiled as softly, secretly as the lip of a pool. Beside her, I saw a wolf with ears bent at the tips, and then an owl staring, and a man with a sheepish smile.

I took the dirt track leading toward the mountain, up past pastures of sage and yellow flowers, past clumps of juniper, clambering the rock spine of ridges, until the road's ruts deepened, softened, and the engine gasped for air. When I left the car and walked, I could feel by a peculiar tug in my ribs that oxygen was short. My trudge slowed, and the splintered white stone of the ground brightened before me. Every beetle shone blue. Glimmering ants trailed along, and a blond grass stem bent. An earth crumb glittered on a stone. In a burrow, a spiderweb crumpled a tuft of light.

At the spring, I bent to drink, my hands on the hard damp mud at the pool's rim, where a white tinge lingered as the water dried. The water tasted mineral, and thickened my tongue. I craved that flavor. Earth fed me rain. I worked upward through scrub, over long scree slopes to the saddle, and along the ridge through thickets of trees toward the summit. The sticks of my bones were squeaking, and my heart drummed high. Cliffs fell away below me, and I tasted the elixir of vertigo.

The hazy flats of Wyoming reached out below. Maybe that was Polecat Bench, that gray line to the north. And that must have been the ridge where the Nez Perce disappeared, rising snowy to the northwest. South, I studied the wrinkled distances I would travel sometime after dark that night. At my feet, gray rock scattered toward the brink, a dead drop farther than I could see without leaning.

The signal station on the summit was a camper shell that must have been helicoptored to where it perched on a pinnacle, tethered with steel cable bolted to rock. Pulling open the stubby aluminum door, I crawled inside to escape the wind and sun. Batteries were harnessed together with wire, weeping acid, keeping the signal alive. And on the bench lay a white flag some climber had left, where everyone since had penned their names, real, fake, prophetic:

Elvis Presley, Powell, Wyo.
I laughed
I cried
It became a part of me
   8/12/1991

Make love not war

Ronald Reagan
7/20/86

Bullet (Nick's dog)

Mary "Touch of gray" McCormack
8/28/47-87: 40!!

Sean Good
we stayed all night

Josh Woodruff
9-2-87

Randy "Crazy Legs" Richard

Rem Oler, age 7

Fran Moreno, Madrid, Spain
  *Aqui estuvo se Vikingo Ruegen*
  *por su alma* † 1983

My dad's a fag

The flag went limp in my hand, and I set it down. A wedge of sunlight crossed the floor where the door twitched. I closed my eyes, and the cables that held this box in place hummed, and wind bent the trees until they muttered. On the ceiling of my mind, all the tracks of my people bristled like constellations: furrows of the city in the dust, the snake of water following the ditch, Bob Woodruff's finger tracing the ridges of history, ruts of the road, the woman and wolf on the barn's sloping tin, the print of my boot at the mud of the spring, and the terse hieroglyphics of the flag. My people have many ways to leave word.

In my back pocket, I felt the hank of barbwire I had wrenched from the fallen fence at the internment camp. I eased it out and set it on the flag on the floor. Then I took out everything: a quarter, my watch with its stubs from a broken plastic band, my notebook and pen, an aspirin dressed in lint, my knife, my wallet and comb. I opened all nine blades of the knife. It bristled in the sun, with its awl, its corkscrew, screwdriver, scissors, stainless blades and gadgets. At the little shrine of my things, I wanted to solve sorrow. If it could all be simple as heads or tails, I could turn over loneliness and find plain solitude. But it wouldn't turn. My knife could slash, pry open, magnify, but it could not solve. I looked out the stubby doorway to a twisted pine, and then a thickening haze of blue that reached the horizon. I felt clenched in the fist of the place. We call it Heart Mountain, but we don't know why.

# Intrusion at Wind River

THE VISION QUEST MOTEL slowed me in Meeteetse, looming from the dark with a promise of rest. But I gathered speed and went on along state highway 120 south to find a sleeping place in the open country. The car hummed steady. The stars glittered thick at the top of the windshield. A long swoop of dark valley, the jumbled heaps of stone that flickered at the edge of my headlights, the wind whistle at the window as I rushed along all said keep moving, don't stop in town, but seek a privacy of sage.

I had fueled my body on beef at Irma's Hotel, in Cody, had fed at a corner table as I studied the cherrywood bar Queen Victoria gave to Buffalo Bill. With its scrolls and mirrors, the supple turnings of the wood spoke the queen's wish, through the keen chisels of her carpenters, to a cowboy's belly sliding at the rail as he reached for a brew. I gnawed my steak, sweetened with salt. Behind me, a farmer was telling his buddy about dry weather.

"I had to pull off the road," he said, "just short of Worland yesterday, to dig a hole in the dirt, reach my hand in, and feel how dry it is this year. It's dry, I'm telling you. I don't like it this dry. I don't care how much water comes down the ditch. If the land's this dry we're all in trouble."

My water glass sweated cold. I thought of that man reaching shoulder-deep into the earth to tickle water up. The roots of grass reach down like hair to gather wet. And he reached down. As I listened to his story, I reached for something, too.

Driving, I reached to tap the dashboard four times for luck. The dark wind whistled at the wind wing. I was humming an old song, a blues. Behind the tune, companion memory told me things: the Vison Quest, the cherrywood bar, the taste of salt, the farmer's hand in dust. And the song worked to thread it all together:

> Cradlewood and coffinwood, they're all the same to me,
> They're both carved out of that same fine tree,
> Oh, losing is an easy game.

But I wasn't losing. I had lost. And now I was on the loose and rambling. Driving nights without a particular destination other than sleep has always been a kind of blessing for me. Some road would beckon, and I would know it. Instead of a map, I counted on moments of knowing. And somewhere past where the road went west for Grass Creek, I turned off on a dark thin track, left my car, slept on a knoll. Dew came first to my sleeping bag, then frost. Sage glimmered pale by starlight all around me, and flavored my rest. I took many turnings on the gritty hard ground, heard the rustle and swoop of night creatures, passed through the torn and mended veil of dreams. Once, when I rolled over and looked up at the stars, I thought I understood how the old Indian women must have learned beadwork there, where the little worlds scatter and turn. Then a line of light eased back the stars. I was standing up to face four ways, shivering barefoot, happy to be that hungry. All around me the good land rose up. Driving, I left my window open and sipped wind. As I came down the slope toward Thermopolis, I saw a shaggy, long-maned pony wagging his big head as he scratched his neck on the barb wire. Sometimes it's hard to explain to someone else just what pleasure is. No one else knows what it takes.

In the Manhattan Cafe at Thermopolis, the man beside me had made his peace with hate. He hated everything in a comfortable, old companion sort of way. I could see it in his face, as his glance darted about the room.

"Goddam forest fires," he said to no one. He crackled his newspaper. "In the spring, too. God damn." I asked him to pass the cream, and became his audience.

"Goddam coffee," he said, looking in my eyes, "I wish I didn't drink it, because when it's bad it makes me sorry." He folded his newspaper, took a sip of coffee, and grimaced. "Where you from?" he said, the grimace lingering on his face.

"Out in Oregon," I said.

"I lived in God damned Klamath Falls," he said, "for a year. Is Oregon all like that?"

"No."

"Well, that's a blessing," he said. "I'm heading home to Nebraska. With this drought, I'll probably find my spread fried to a plain white. You want my sausage?"

"No, thank you."

"Grease'll kill you," he said. "Don't know why I ordered it." He opened his paper again, read a few column inches, scanned the page, hurled it shut. "Want my paper?" he said.

"Sure," I said. "Thanks." I folded the paper into a strip, sipped my coffee. It was wonderfully bitter and thin. "Who's minding the ranch," I said, "while you're gone?"

"My head wetback," he said, crackling open a packet of sugar. "He's been working spring season for me ten years. A God damn good hand." He poured half the sugar into his coffee, spilled the rest, lowered his wide mouth to blow the counter clean. Poof! "He knows cattle," he said, "and he knows my ranch. Keeps the wells pumping, or trucks water out to the stock tanks if they fail."

"Cream?" I said.

"Just sugar," he said. "Damn poor excuse for coffee."

"And summers he goes home to Mexico?"

"Yeah, he goes. Lately I've taken to driving him back. I got relatives work my place summers, and they get on my damn nerves, so I leave them in Nebraska and drive him back to Mexico. He has a spread of his own down out of Chihuahua. He's up a valley in the mountains there, just enough water to keep it green. He's got more mountain on his little ranch than the whole damn state of Nebraska. We work his herd into the high country, up where it's cool. God damn good life in there."

"So you trade?"

"We trade," he said. "It all works out." His lips curled back. "He's a good man. Damn coffee."

"Take it easy," I said, took my newspaper, and went away.

At the park east of town, on their fenced hill, the captive wild buffalo grazed on feed pellets. The sign said not to leave your car. I got out. I wanted to hear them breathe. Hear their hooves stamp dust. I wanted to look down at my own feet, then let my gaze sweep directly across the blond prairie grass to where they stood, a few steps up the hill, a tableau. A buffalo cow lay down heavy in a rush of dust, her calf bounding out of the way. The little eyes of the old bull glittered. I took two steps forward. He swung his head away to see me better. What did he remind me of, parking his bulk against the sky like that? He had a heavy glint to his eye. His glance was steel. I've met people who should have been wild, but were too damn lazy to break the fence.

At the south edge of town, I couldn't resist stopping at Grandma's Liquor Store, not to buy, but to meet grandma, ask her something. I glanced at a sign by the road there, "The Wedding of the Waters," and jangled through the door.

"Howdy," I said, "how's business?"

"You're my first," she said. She put her palms on the counter, tilted her head back to study me with friendly gray eyes. She looked like the kind of grandma who could start another family, if she took a fancy, or tell the family she already had to go get lost.

44

"Why," I said, "do they call this place 'The Wedding of the Waters'?"

"Oh," she said, "on account the name of the river changes. Wind River turns into the Bighorn there at the mouth of the canyon."

"How'd they decide to do that?"

"I don't know," she said, "it's been that way a good long time. Well, though, maybe I do know. When you get married, or unmarried, know how you meet a change? That must be what they meant."

I changed my mind and bought a palm-sized flask of Jack Daniels. "Keep happy," she said, taking my money, and sprinkling change into my palm. My fingers crackled the brown paper at the bottle's neck as I jangled out the door.

Where the first ramparts of the canyon rose from the river, I parked in the shade and climbed, up past caves with wisps of owl down, scrambling up the talus, the scree, the bluffs, to the rim. A sign by the road had told me the age of this rock. I tried to remember: a million years? Three million? A billion? Was that the sign that told of volcanic intrusions in sedimentary strata? Even rock had an adventurous biography. The land was formed when stone burned. Wind nudged me at the edge. I heard a slap of water, another. Down there, at the far edge of the river, in the shallows, some big fish was walking. Its back glistened, and its fins frisked the mud. Then it thrashed back to deep water. That fish seemed older than rock, older than any sign could name. But then I thought again, and grandma's humor seemed oldest of all. Things bent and lived.

On south, punching into the sudden gash of the Wind River canyon, I felt like a tiny bug piercing the fossil depths of the world. My silverfish car dove busy into the quiet heart of the earth, where rock rose tier on tier toward the blue. The long curves swung me outward, snug against the seatbelt harness, steady, then logic tilted me over, my body shifted and I leaned the other way, veering wide where the river led the road. Leaning like that at sixty, I felt how the river hurls a fish, how a running deer clears the fence with one staccato burst of hooves and a bound, how the wind swings the swallow down and out against the shudder of its wings. My fingers gripped the little knobs of the wheel. Sweat cooled my head.

I swung south, paused in Shoshoni for a milkshake, then swung west. The country opened flat and hot, and I couldn't keep my feet off it. I had to leave the car, where a lone hill beckoned. Sand slowed my steps. A hot wind drew me to the shade of a bluff, and I reached into a low cave to take up a coyote skull where the ants had left it clean. The teeth fit perfectly shut. I read poison in that scatter of bones. But the wind was sweet and clean, and the bones were clean. Poison must have salted the killer's hands.

Maybe the cool of the cave's breath, with the sun hot on my back, brought sudden to mind those three lithe girls making my fresh peach shake at the Yellowstone Drug in Shoshoni. They had worked so smoothly as one—one curled over, her belly against the chrome of the counter, delving deep into the cold bin to scoop out hard ice cream; and one pouring an arc of milk into the tall steel can, tapping it down, pouring again till it foamed; and one spooning fresh peach slivers into the can, and running the lime green Hamilton Beach milkshake spinner, working the steel can up and down to shatter every blob of ice and pour it smooth into a glass, clank down the can on the counter beside it and smile.

"One fresh peach served." She had looked into my eyes, tilted her head to the side. And then, wringing her hands in a towel, she had turned to her friends with scoop and carton. "Hey, how'd the prom go for Lorretta in Riverton?"

The shake chilled me to the bone. I drained the last white drops. Outside, painted ten feet tall on the wall of a business that failed, a brutal face of Geronimo grinned down.

At the cave, I set down the coyote skull in its exact dust print. The milkshake had fattened me. The quick bright life of the girls had filled me. Out on the flat, the hot sun on my back fingered into my body, and a warm breeze, with its hint of sage pollen and sun-bruised stone, gathered into me breathing deep. I felt close to that desert place, for I had waked on the land. I had met a stranger and learned his story by the thin flavor of bad coffee. I had met grandma, watched the old fish walk, sipped the chill cream girls gave me, touched bone. It felt so easy to be content. I was going to Jackson, sometime later that day. The roads all connected. I would figure it out.

The road was going where I wanted. Its ribbon led me. A pickup passed me, piled high with hay bales and a dog on top with its nose to the wind. I passed a long-maned woman on a white horse running. My heart ran, and her hair flickered. Willow bush heaved and swayed like flame. Mirage splashed at the south horizon. I burned gas and the whole land seemed to run with me. My drug was travel and my food was wind. I passed the block house with red letters on the side: "Wild game cutting, wrapping, caping to go." Pickup trucks nosed in at the rail. And in the fields, water scattered from sprinklers, glittered in ditches. I passed through Riverton, and picked up speed. I entered the Wind River Indian Reservation, felt the light thicken. Sage blurred into banners on both sides of the road, trailed behind me.

I passed the crest of noon, started down the far side. The sun glanced through my windshield aiming west. I squinted, and colors drained from the land. A scatter of bones whitened the ditch. A long hill guarded a crescent of shadow. A house had no door. The wind had pried back tin from a shed roof, would strip it. The sage land passed me for miles without a change, without a decision. Distance was the major topographical feature. Now and then there was a human syllable of wire or twin road rut. Then sage.

Somewhere out there I passed a floral silk robe flapping in the wind where it had snagged on a barb wire gate in the wide open middle of nowhere.

A glittering line of color called me off the road at St. Stephens. The heat of midafternoon slicked the horizon with mirage, not like a shimmer of water, but of the hot wind congealed. Willow leaves hung limp. The ground's white dust punished my eyes. I walked toward the Arapaho cemetery where ribbons and plastic flowers twitched, where the colors on the crosses dazzled blood red and sky blue, where the names were writ three times: an Arapaho name, an English translation, an alternate common name. It was all hand work, and cleanly made. *White Shirt. Bear Woman. Vietnam Vetran.*

I stood by the cross for Thomas Shakespeare III a long time. The sun overhead had gleaned every softness. All colors burned exact. River rocks, salted with alkali, ringed his grave. A stunted whirlwind snatched up plastic flowers, spun them past me. I was listening.

A pickup truck bounced slowly over the field, squeaked to a halt. A woman climbed out, then two children, then a man. They came to the grave two graves away from where I stood, the grave of a girl and a boy, together. I could see it had been vandalized, the glass vase broken, flowers scattered. The children from the truck, girl and boy, scampered and laughed. The woman stood still, then began to swear. She called with a wail to the children.

"Come here now! Help your cousins! See what someone has done!" She did not look at me. "See what someone has felt they could do to your cousins." She turned her back to me. "See what someone from far away who does not understand has done." The boy jumped over a stone in the path, heedless, and she struck the boy at the side of his head. "I am talking to you," she said, "and you do not listen." The girl suddenly became still, clasped her hands over her belly. "See," said the woman, "now we have to straighten this." She grabbed the girl by the shoulder and shook her toward the grave. "Pick up those things. Put that broken glass in a pile. Get the rake."

The man stood back, looking off toward the horizon. I stared down at the mound of earth over Thomas Shakespeare, the stone ring around him, the wood cross rising up. The tipi rings I had seen on Polecat Bench grew tight around one man, beads around a silence.

"Quickly," the woman said. "The sun burns us." The girl

and boy crouched beside their cousins' graves, stuck the plastic flowers into the dust, gathered the glass slivers into a heap, and stood, looking down. The boy pulled a rake over the sand, smoothing the plot. "Come on," said the woman, turning from them toward the truck, "we're going." She let her gaze sweep past me, trudged away. The children followed her. The man went last.

Their truck drifted away through the haze. It glinted, and was gone. I reached for a deep breath, but it burned. A flag on a veteran's cross twitched, and hung still. The earth lay cracked beside my foot. I felt foreign, withered, odd. Thomas Shakespeare had a right. I had a right. But Thomas had earned his right forever. I had to intrude and pay. I had to accept this woman's anger, stacked in her heart like glass. Maybe she did not speak her anger to the children, or to me, but to my people. I was her messenger, carrying her anger, the hurt secrets of the place.

My car was hot. My engine, cousin to the sun, carried me from the dust of the cemetery road onto the black shimmer of the highway. I passed a farm yard row of thirty fenceposts, each with a cowboy boot shoved top-end down, curling and bleaching in the sun. I remembered hearing how St. Stephens had suffered a run of suicides, young ones. They killed themselves one after another, until everyone was afraid. Children cleaned the graves. Every boot curled on its post. I was a tourist, not understanding anything. I saw it raw, in ignorance. I had no right to understand, for I was running. It was at the cemetery I had started to know why. I had turned west. At Shoshoni, I had ended my rambling, and turned back toward the house in Oregon where I felt magnetically repelled. I fought it. I wanted to turn around, and leave my tracks backward in the dust of the cemetery, back into the willows, turn once around and keep going somewhere so no one could find me.

But I drove west. I took out my watch, my $3 Timex with its broken band. The busiest hand was the color of blood. By each number, a dot of radium waited for night. The knurled brass knob was worn so smooth I had to wind it with pliers.

I had to travel hard. I would be late in Jackson. The car swung me past a silver-boarded house, a dry wash, bleached pasture, long flat of open land. Something pressed against my heart. Suffocation. Driving west, I felt something closing in. I couldn't stay in the car. I was late, but I turned off the highway to a smaller road.

Beyond Ethete, at Fort Washakie I sat on the top fence rail to watch the end of the weekend rodeo, where the three-lap bareback relay race ran last. At the pistol shot, two young riders leaped onto their ponies, slapped hard and thundered around the track, low and smooth on the far side, then out of sight behind the fence at the bend, then back around, careening to the start to bound off in one jump and leap on another horse, ears up then tail flat out and gone. I felt the joy of their punishment, wanting to run that much. At the final lap, the winning horse whirled at the finish, staggered, limped, the rider turning away.

At Crowheart I stopped to call the woman I had married seventeen years before. I tried long distance at the vacant gas station's phonebooth. No answer. Something far away tried ringing, ringing. By my hand, wind riffled the yellow pages, brittle and dry. I hoped she would not answer. I got my wish.

West from Dubois, climbing out of the heat, I came to the high cold country on the slant of the Great Divide, and I babbled to the hum of the engine. Fatigue had hit. Homeless hurt closed in. I had this ragbag of sensations from the day. So what? How long had it been since I touched anyone? In the morning, I had felt well fed, had savored the pulse of the wind. Now, my life felt like a stray ricochet, aimless and fast. I spoke to my hand, knotted before my lips. I chattered, grumbled, bitched. Something had to change. There is pain, and then there is too much pain.

At that altitude, it was the time in early spring when no leaves block the view. I scanned the bright red of willow stems, the beginnings of a river ripping at the bank, gray rock. Over the top, I took my foot off the gas and coasted down.

Winter had bruised the place. It mostly had melted away, but I could see how trees had been bent and shattered by heavy snow. I felt kin to the dusty twist of each trunk. The wind turned cold. A little snow sifted down. I knew two things. I would love my daughter. I would live. There was just enough haze of light snow falling to soften the green of the pines.

# Everything We Have

AT THE 24-HOUR ELKHORN CAFE IN JACKSON I studied the
rogues' gallery on the wall, a grid of oil portraits where rugged
men in their barnwood frames stared me down. What kind of
man was I? What kind of man would say goodby so soon? She
had moved like a river across the room, out through the door
to the dark. Her cup sat empty at my table, in a scatter of
crumbs. Maybe I sent her away with something in my voice,
when I decided to be alone. Or maybe it was too dangerous for
both of us, and we knew it, and made a pact to walk away
from what we wanted.

The Elkhorn air was tinged with smoke. A steak sizzled in
the kitchen. I turned the tines of my fork down, printed its
four claws into the napkin in a pattern like falling snow. A
wisp of steam rose from my empty cup. What now? My friend
had told me remedies for feeling lost. In her quiet voice,
everything seemed secret and true. She had a way of turning
her head, saying a few words, and a thought came bumping
sideways into my mind. In winter, she had said, sometimes you
just have to follow your own tracks home. Then she had
shaken her long hair aside and something hurt me with

longing. Seeing her, I longed for more life, more words like these, I wanted touch, this laughter. I had almost reached to touch her sleeve, but in her eyes I saw that something made her afraid, and I believed it was me. Out under the stars now somewhere, she was walking home.

In my room at the Executive Inn, I closed the curtains and lay flat. The pillow starched my face like canvas. Streetlight through a curtain slit hit the back wall above me. In my silent room, the busy TV world awaited my command, behind its curved belly of glass. All it took was the touch of a knob. The telephone, cradled by the bed, could connect me with everyone I knew. Did I know anyone, at this time of night? In the drawer by my bed I found the Gideon Bible with a giddy note some honeymooner had scribbled on the inside cover: "Sweet love and dancing all night long you do." Then I delved into the book for prophecy, found a good one somewhere: "For every creature of God is good, and nothing to be refused, if it be received with thanksgiving." I had to rumple through my heap of clothes on the chair to find my notebook and write that down. If I kept it, maybe someday I could act that with my life. A book of matches lay centered in an ashtray. I clicked off the light. Staring at the glittered ceiling, I counted the cars going past outside, muffled by snow on the roads. Nothing to be refused. In the mountains, maybe, the snow came down like her hair moved.

Next morning when I visited the high school, my students told me the message James Watt, local rancher and former Secretary of the Interior, had delivered to them that morning. In his lecture on "Morality and the Constitution," he had affirmed that conservation of natural resources is a waste of time because the world will be destroyed very soon. "And what did you say to him?" I asked them. "We told him he's crazy." I felt a thrill. This was useful information to me because I was to be the luncheon speaker at the Rotary Club later that day, where Mr. Watt was a member. Our whole country, I thought, has to follow its own tracks home. Even me.

After class, I left the high school parking lot in a swirl of snow, and found my way to the Rotary's motel banquet room, the windowless chamber with folding walls where Rotarians milled and sidled through flocks of folding chairs crouched around tables set with chrome and china. Everywhere, friends were meeting, pointing and grinning, with a happy backslap kinship. They had a good thing going, and they knew it. Someone showed me to the head table, and I sipped water, nibbled lettuce, looked up from my chicken into the eyes of the tall man a nametag labeled James Watt. He looked like someone's uncle. I realized I didn't just need to talk to him. I needed to talk to everyone, every life in the room. I studied the placard by my plate, the Rotary International Four-Way Test of the things we think, say, or do, the specific tests of a life to put service above self:

1. Is it the *truth*?
2. Is it fair to all concerned?
3. Will it build *Goodwill* and *Better Friendships*?
4. Will it be *Beneficial* to all concerned?

Do I do that—say something twice without quite saying what I mean? I believe I do. Lunch was done, the games and fines and ribbing, and the program chairman stepped to the podium to introduce me.

"Our speaker today, he said, "is a poet." Members here and there glanced at their watches, pushed their chairs back, reached for their briefcases. The chairman put on his glasses and began to read, "Our speaker comes from Oregon, where he is director of the Northwest Writing Institute, and holds a Ph.D. in medieval literature." I could see a desperate look in the eyes of several men in sharp black suits near the front, but the chairman went on without mercy. "He has published a book called *Having Everything Right*, which I haven't read, but our librarian tells me it's excellent, and I see he has brought his guitar. Please welcome Dr. Kim R. Stafford." When I rose to speak, there was a clatter of glassware, muffled by applause, and a scraping of chairs as the busiest members departed. I waited for the room to settle, stood silent a moment before the shiny little grill of the microphone, then launched into a story for the scattered Rotarians who remained.

"I stopped at Irma's," I said, "in Cody, and I heard two farmers talking about dry weather. One said he had been driving along toward Worland, and he felt the call to stop and dig himself a hole in the dust, just to reach down into the earth and see how dry it was. It was dry, he said, and that troubled him. I think the makers of stories do that for all of us—reaching into the dark of the human spirit to seek the water that gives us life. Children reach down, and dreams reach down. We learn young that you have to struggle for truth, for fairness, for friendship that can last and change. . . ."

At this point, the oldest among them, the one with the nametag "Homer," who sat hunched in the front row fiddling constantly with his phone-sized hearing aid, struggled to his feet. Someone helped prop him up, and the room fell still. I put a hand over my notes, and looked down into his eyes. He wrestled with the words, but got them out in a fervent tangle: "If, if, if we had more Rotary clubs, we'd have, we'd have no wars!" He sat down.

I stood still, stunned by the man. "Yes," I finally whispered, holding my lips close to the microphone, "thank you." I scrambled through my notes. I believed him, and wanted to shout, to join him, or to sit down and let my elders speak. What could follow his demand? My mouth kept talking about something, and I guess my hands fumbled for the guitar. Homer started adjusting the dials on his hearing aid, making it squeak. James Watt sat straight, and I talked. There is a seamless moment deep inside when I stand at the podium, where I can hear my voice talking, biding time, trying to hold the room in a polite trance. I can see the faces, the silverware, the glasses sweating chill, and yet I am somewhere far inside the den of myself, taking counsel. Is it time to sing something sweet, a thing for easy rest, a tune to heal the hurt? Or is it time to challenge, to hurt complacency? My oldest self said hurt. Then my speaking voice was saying the cowboy's prayer, as my arms cradled the guitar. And then my fingers were work- ing the strings, and my voice was sliding into my ballad of the homeless hitchhiker I had picked up years before, the man who told me the story of his car burning with everything he had.When the guitar chords started, my Ph.D. was nothing and I was a Rotarian, and we all were a company on the road together with this vagabond.

No song should end without some kind of mercy,
No one's life should be like this song.
But mine has been and you who listen,
Bless your luck. So long.

Something caught me by surprise in the song, caught my voice in a tangle like Homer's voice. Suddenly the song was true in a way I hadn't known. I was homeless, and all my pleasures had burned. I looked down helplessly into the eyes of James Watt, of Homer, and I searched the crowd. Far inside, the voice said Keep Going. I kept putting syllables in front of each other un- til I was done. My voice said a last word somehow, and my mouth shut.

After the program, as members were leaving through exit doors on all sides, James Watt among the foremost, I stepped toward Homer to thank him. When I entered the narrow arena of his attention, he fixed me with a hawkish stare, gripped my wrist, and whispered fiercely.

"In just a little while," he wheezed, "All we have will be taken from us!" He tightened his grip. I could feel the bones of his fingers against my pulse. "And two-hundred years," he whispered, "is just a little while!" His gaze found my center. He tossed my hand down like a rag, the light in his eyes receded, and his helper led him away.

Everything we have? All the doors had opened, and sud- denly the room was cold. I felt a desperate haste to love, to say all, to snatch up the strands of my life, braid them snug some- how. The plastic handle to my guitar case felt like shaped ice.

In my room at the Executive that afternoon, I could do nothing but sing, clamp my fingers through their changes on the guitar strings, until the fretted dents in my fingerprints ached. I heard the TV telling stories in the next room, could not make out the words, but felt the tug and moan behind the words, a woman's. Everything we have will be taken from us. What did I have beyond longing? I had a daughter I loved. But she lived in a house where I couldn't live, and I was teaching her wrong by living sad.

I went out and wandered the snowy streets, clambered over ice where the snowplow had piled it. Windows displayed fur, carved bone, crystals, purple cloth. In the eyes of women I saw rivers of sun. Everything we have. The wind fingered my neck, and I turned in through a door. In the Million Dollar Cowboy Bar, I overheard half a story of betrayal as I sipped my coffee: "She got so she couldn't go home, like the doorknob was too hot to touch." I felt a snarl in the pit of my belly. So true. I had to go out again, walk this cold from my body, stamp it into the ground. On the boardwalk, I picked up a scrap of paper torn from the Jackson entertainment guide, and paused to read it:

> The White Buffalo. According to Sioux Indian lore, those who glimpse this rare and sacred creature become members of an elite group. The White Buffalo Supper Club carries on this tradition of distinction with exceptional dining in a truly elegant atmosphere....

The paper suddenly became small in my fist. The streets were darkening, the lit storefront windows turning gold. I set off along an alley. The backs of buildings seemed honest, with here and there a scrap roof of rusted tin, cobweb windows, trash. No one tried to sell my culture to me there. A little snow came sifting down, and my feet crunched frozen slush. Then I slowed. A great collection huddled under a roof. There were half bicycles, chests of drawers, chairs stacked upside down, a cross, a welcome sign, and a cluster of silent men staring at me. I turned toward them, and found myself walking through a back door, the front door of Orville's, the homeless shelter squirreled away behind the theater at the heart of this resort town. Impulse had me, and I felt welcome. Steam spiraled from the kitchen kettle, and everyone shuffled around with their hands in their pockets.

"I'm just here," said one man to another, "because my sister aint got room for more than my wife and kids. Come job, we'll be alright."

"Yeah," said the other, "yeah." The smokers came stamping in from the porch, where they had been leaning on old refrigerators and talking softly. No one asked me what I needed. We didn't much look each other in the eye. The man who looked everyone in the eye, he must have been Orville himself. I smiled. He didn't need to. His face accepted me and the other travelers.

It wasn't long before I was lining up for spaghetti with the forty guests of the place. From their backs, I learned how to shuffle, raise one shoulder. The forks of the seated throng scraped fiercely at their plates. Scotty, the keeper of the thrift store, had just been telling Orville his great triumph.

"See, I had this old Royal portable on the shop shelf for months? Months! What a beauty: gold script on the body, and gold on all the keys. But no one showed the least interest. Then I rolled in a sheet of paper, typed 'On this typewriter, Ernest Hemingway wrote his first short story.' And you know?" He snapped his fingers. "It sold like *that!*"

Scotty picked me out from the crowd, a new face, and he escorted me to what he called The Hemingway Chair, and set down a tumbler of punch and a heaped plate of pasta in front of me.

"Eat like no tomorrow," he said. "There's always a tomorrow at Orville's, but you're traveling." Scotty and Orville took seats at my table, and pretty soon everyone was lost in the busy warmth of the meal. As I shoveled and dug at the spaghetti, I began to tell Scotty and Orville about my near meeting with James Watt.

"I gave him Badger Clark's 'Cowboy's Prayer,'" I said, "then sang my ballad of the homeless man."

Orville looked at me. "You sing?" he said.

"I try what I can with my three chords."

A woman at the next table turned toward us. "Sir," she said softly, "will you sing for us what you sang for him?"

"I'm afraid," I said, "I have a pretty raspy voice without my old guitar."

Orville turned to the woman. "Roe, why don't you get that guitar you just bought, your Stella, and let our guest sing for us?" She was gone up the stairs in a flash, and returned with her guitar, holding it out as something revered but foreign, exotic, alive.

"I bought this," she said, "from Scotty. But I can't play it. Will you, sir?" As I took the guitar in my arms, a man beside me with greasy hands and neither luggage nor coat pulled a guitar pick out of his hip pocket and handed it to me. I thanked him, and thanked Roe, and tinkered with my three chords, and then sang the story of the hitchhiker as James Watt never heard it:

"It's a wonder we're together
When the times get so low.
Some like us soon go under."
"Some like us, oh I suppose."

There was a polite din of forks scraping plates as I sang, of the cook in the kitchen rattling pans, and there was something else, a hush of sympathy, of the homeless company living with the lost man in the song. Out of the corner of my eye, I could see Orville turning his spoon over and over, as he bowed his head to ponder. I could see Roe, with her head thrown back so her eyes shone, and Scotty hunched on his elbows and sporting a grin. The man with greasy hands had set his face hard, so hard and still his eyes flickered, and his long look showed the play of memory soft and vivid as a movie screen. Maybe you have to lose everything to be so generous in the way you take a gift, an episode of song, a moment together like that.

And then the last chord, the last syllable closed, and the room came to life. Orville ordered everyone outside, Roe took her guitar away, a hand reached and opened for the guitar pick, there was a flurry of tables cleared, and everyone was gone to the streets until bedtime.

"Come see us anytime," said Orville, closing the door behind me. I watched the forty scatter away along the alley, clambering over the heaps of frozen snow. A cold fog dimmed the streetlight. I clambered after them.

In the Elkhorn Cafe late that night, I took out my tiny notebook to lecture myself, recording what sleeplessness had to say. Maybe Homer had a code like this, and maybe Orville did, and maybe the friend I loved:

> Live alone. Take the small nourishment of passing friendship when you find it. Treat it generously & with care. Seek in the writing & telling the intimacy you cannot find in life. Your home is in the travel, still homesick for the road. This feeling now—of longing, uncertainty, and hope—this is home. Be strong enough to live in this. Help others. Meeting the bear is nothing to this chain of years.

I put the notebook back in the pocket by my heart, took a deep, stale breath. What now? By dawn, my car was creeping west over the steep hump of Teton Pass toward Victor, Swan Valley, and Idaho.

# New Heaven and New Earth

WITH A SHORT WHEEZE AND A RATTLE, my car coasted to zero at the boundary of the Fort Hall Indian Reservation in Idaho. After a pause, listening to the wind, I got it started and crept up the ramp to a station, where the engine shrieked and died again. I tried cranking the engine, but it made a terrible squeal. A mechanic from the Sho-Ban tribe leaned his elbows on the radiator and listened to the shriek, then shook his head at me.

"Sounds bad," he said. "Oil pump, maybe. Better get towed to Pocatello." He helped me push the car away from the station pumps, and we left it in the shade of a kneeling semi waiting for a tire. The afternoon was warm. I felt my shoulders sag, and then I straightened and looked at the sky. Fat clouds moved east. The parking lot stretched wide and damp with rain. Across from the gas station, beyond a glitter of car windshields, lay the food market, the post office, and the tribal trading post. I called Pocatello at the pay phone, gritted my teeth when they quoted me a fee, told them to come get me, then hung up. While I waited, I let my intuition lead, and sidled into the trading post for the fragrance of smoke-tanned buckskin, and to savor the dazzle of beads.

A lit showcase lined the south and east walls to display beaded purses and wallets and buckles, rectangular buckles with geometric design for a man, and oval buckles with roses beaded petal, leaf, and stem for a woman. There were palm-sized barrettes dizzy with color for the long hair of Shoshone women, Bic pens beaded blue, moccasins beaded heel to toe, white doeskin gloves with beaded eagles at the cuffs. I asked to see the raw beads, and the woman brought out boxes, long slim boxes filled with tiny glass beads eight to the inch, twelve, sixteen. She lifted out a few strands, let them run through her fingers. When I saw the crimson cut beads, the faceted ones that glittered, I wanted them. Want had a taste, a tingle in my throat, at my wrists, my belly. With no plan or excuse but the thrill I felt, I bought beads, white-threaded hanks of blue and red, pink and moss green beads. My car had given out, and my life was not going well, but the beads were fine. I didn't want the whole thing finished, not buckle, not glove. I wanted the beads.

Then the tow truck came, I stowed the beads, climbed in beside the driver, and got towed back to Pocatello. We backed my old car into a repair shop on Yellowstone Drive. The tow truck roared away with the fiery arrogance of a young engine. An old fellow named Elmer Bushta reached his dipstick stethoscope into my engine, and twirled his finger for me to crank it once. A squeal from the crankshaft made him wave his hand in alarm. He stuck his head in beside me to peer at the odometer, squinted, straightened, and wiped off his hands.

"Are you sure," he said, "this engine has really gone 289,000 miles?" I nodded. He raised his eyebrows to accept this fact, and tipped his head as a kind of respectful greeting to the car. Then he rolled the computer diagnostic unit to the car's flank, and twirled its knobs. I read their names from where I sat inside: Primary Current, Dwell, Kill, Remote Kill, Parade, Stack, Shift, Freeze. But then Elmer thought better of cranking the engine even one more time. He said he would have to break it down, and I should check back in a few days.

I took my pack from the car and handed Elmer the keys.

Outside the shop, a bumper sticker on a parked car spoke for me: "Heaven doesn't want me, and Hell's afraid I'll take over." I wanted to take over this town. There was a glory to its debris and spunky hope, a seasoned character. I set out at a hungry clip, hungry for the thirty-year standstill of old downtown. And right away, around the corner, I couldn't resist wandering into a bowling alley, just to give my soul a wake-up shock. The door is always glass, framed in aluminum, and when you swing it open the burly whirl of the place comes at you in a rush. I savored the rattling crush of demolished pins, the gleaming lawn of green linoleum, the blur of smoke and din and blue team blazers. A woman danced at the line, teetering wild on one foot to keep her careening ball from the gutter, but there it went. Clunk. She laughed as she whirled to face her friends.

She fit the place, and her laugh fit her. I remembered a shepherd I had glimpsed north of Dayton, where he rested in the sage as I spun past. He and his dog lay on the earth more perfectly than I had ever seen. And now I watched an old man's companionship with his bowling ball, as he turned it, rolled it in the rack to seek the three-finger hold that fit him like rings. When his fingers found their hold, he lifted it out, and his smile made his cigarette twitch and shake ash.

But it was April 15 and I was out of socks, so I slipped on down the street to the laundromat to run a load and do my taxes. Not much crowd, just a lady in curlers with a little bitty load, and a young woman pretty as a bride with sheets and towels in a mound. I pushed a pile of damp magazines to the side and spread my paperwork on the formica coffee table, then hauled my pack of clothes to the side-loader, filled it, fed it soap and quarters, punched the long-cycle button, the cold-cold option, and hit start. It churned, and I started through my forms.

Right away I found out I'd had 37 employers, 13,580 business miles on my car, and 78 travel days in the previous year. I'd have a hard time fitting it all to the lines on the forms. But when I turned to the forms themselves, it was the filing status that stalled me. Should it be single, or married filing joint return, or married filing separate? The IRS asked such elemental questions.

"I wouldn't put those in together, if I was you," said the woman in curlers to the bride. "Your darks will stain your lights." The younger woman hesitated where she stood on her toes to lower a husky pair of jeans into her machine.

"I don't mean to pry, honey," the woman continued, "but I saw you putting negligee in there, and that won't last with the jeans. Here, let's get his things in another machine." She took the jeans by the cuffs, and led them to the mouth of another side-loader, and the bride lowered them in. "It just works better this way," said the woman, glancing at me, "take my word."

Pretty soon all our machines were spinning and gurgling. The bride read a magazine, the woman scanned the bulletin board, and I bent over my desk. I studied the language of my form, its list of life doings: security, penalty, partnership. The forms wondered about my health, my death. The forms hankered after my gross income, my gains or losses, royalties, tips, child, household, widow, home. I started adding figures on the backs of envelopes, scribbled a year's expenses until the pencil dulled, shaved it to a new fine point with my knife, and started on income: profit, accrual, returns, interest, bad debts, depletion, depreciation, cost, cash. I figured my penalty for underpayment of estimated tax by individuals and fiduciaries. I followed the suggested plan: "number of days on line 24b, divided by 366, times 11, times underpayment on line 22 (see instructions)." My washer clicked off. I lugged my wet bundle to the dryer, slid the temp range to hot, and fed dimes to the slot. With a groan that sang to a whine, the dryer drum spun to a start, and my shirts went whirling and snapping their buttons against the sides of the steel drum.

The two women sat side by side now, reading magazines: *People* and *Family Circle*. The woman with curlers closed hers first. She turned just slightly toward the bride.

"Where did you two meet?" she said.

"At a dance."

"And what does he do?"

"Construction. He's good at lots of things."

There was a loud shake and thudding from the machines, as they hit the hard spin cycle, and I missed a few lines, then the woman went on.

"Will you two make your home here in Pocatello," she said, "or will you try another place?"

"He says it's too early to say."

"But when the children come. . . ."

"He says it's too early to say about that, too. We don't have to decide that yet."

The woman with curlers tilted her head, put down her magazine. "Sometimes people don't decide," she said. "It just happens before they think."

"I know that," said the bride, "I've seen it with my friends." She giggled. "Before they know it, they got tribes."

"It happens, honey." The woman smiled, and lowered her voice, and I bent lower over my forms, straining to hear. "Then sometimes," she said, and I missed some words, then caught the thread: "to your man, and you're left with the little ones." She looked down at her hands. "Then they get bigger," she said. "They just do that. It's hard for a while. And then school's over, or they leave it, and they're gone."

My dryer had stopped. All the dryers had stopped. I opened the door on mine, and put my hand on a damp pair of jeans. Steam came over my face like a fever.

The two women got up to check their clothes, and I slipped a dime in my dryer, and returned to the forms. There on the back of the blank 1040, I found my wife's signature in blue. It turned around and around itself like a lint thread tangled on the page. There was a time I found it pretty, turning like a river, or the wind. Something got rinsed out of me since then. Or out of her. Out of us. I entered my guesses on the proper lines, signed the forms, wrote out a pair of checks for my country and my state, and licked my envelopes' peppermint glue. They sealed fat but flat. I slapped on a pair of American flag stamps for each.

The two women were helping each other fold sheets. Watching them, I wanted their friendship to be stronger than marriage, their readiness to help each other through everything. I wanted this chance encounter to become a story of new kinship. The way they looked at each other as they folded those sheets, it went like a dance with wings, and all the machines were still.

I paired my socks, folded my shirts, stuffed everything into my pack, and went out. At the corner, the blue post office box gave a shriek when I tipped open the door. I heard the envelopes give two soft taps before the door slammed shut.

There are times when you can feel the soul of concrete through your shoes with every step, every slap of shoe leather along the sidewalk. I felt it. I felt the heat of my dry clothes through the pack on my back, the heat of the afternoon on my brow. What could I do with a few days in Pocatello, a city haunted with stories? My wife and I had come here six years back, our daughter was born, and we lived that joy in the midst of confusion about where our family path might lie. Arthur Street, where I walked, mapped those days.

Coming back through the old downtown on foot gave me the homeless vagabond's look on it all. I might sleep in the carpeted halls of The Fargo, where I had sometimes stumbled over delerious sleepers when we dwelt there in 1982. I might seek out Austin, the homeless professor who once ghost-wrote student papers for the sheer challenge, perhaps finding him at his unofficial headquarters in the Dead Horse Saloon. I might visit the Toombs sisters, stare at their wall shrine to JFK, and share their chocolates while we listened to their police scanner crackle with static: "Shush! We got a woman passed out in a bowling alley, and we're waiting for the ambulance to get her!" I might prowl the Yellowstone Hotel, the Old Timers Cafe, the rail yard, the ethnic sections of the cemetery, the Greek Orthodox Cathedral, the Harlem Club.

I might seek out that shack on the west side, where a

doctor left a convict's bones to bleach in a barrel of brine, after winning the body in a poker game. Or I might visit the bones themselves, threaded together with wire, they say, where they hang in the high school's biology room. I might drift through the parking lot where my old Chevy came roaring to life after a snow burial of four months. I might crouch by the lilac hedge where I held our daughter in the sun, and she wailed, and I laughed with joy and gratitude.

I remembered the night before our child was born, in the spring of 1982, how we climbed the concrete steps on the hill west of town, clear up to a field where people used to dance by starlight in the old days. Now, I found my way to that place again, climbed the cracked steps where they sagged and heaved on the slope, and at the top I tried to feel that joy and gratitude somewhere in me. We had stood there holding each other, my wife and I, at the boundary of the city's lights, knowing our lives were about to change. The child came, we were a family, on we moved. But there's a strange thing about change: it doesn't stop. Routine can't hold it still.

In the glare of noon, my body felt heavy, climbing the hill. The sun hit me, but in every shadow, frost kept outlines white. The cold air smelled of sage. I stood at the boundary there, at the top of the stairs, which had once been our summit of hope. Behind me, the town seemed to breathe and toil. At the foot of the concrete steps, a street ran north. By the magic and the tyranny of my culture, it connected to every paved path in my country. I had to go forward, go on up the hill through the sage. I had to leave the mapped pattern, and ramble another way.

The ground beckoned me south, bleak with litter and rabbit track in the dust, path and ravine braiding the hillside. After half an hour of stumbling wherever the next path opened, I realized I would come to something I remembered from before, the log cabin built from railroad ties, with its roof of sod, and a set of small frame dwellings. In 1982, I had haunted that place, picking through the litter of other lives, curious about what became of happiness. I had found a blue book in one shack of the compound, a book I remembered as *New Heaven and New Earth*. I remembered reading from it aloud, where I stood in the shack alone, then setting it down in its dust print on the floor.

From the sage now I came onto a road winding up from town, and went on by memory to seek where that tribe had dwelt apart. Where the road ended at a barbwire gate, I saw a crumpled pair of purple panties frozen in the mud. I tried to imagine parking there for love, the coils of barbwire from the busted fence tangled across the road, and the fervent lights of Pocatello pulsing below. Then I bent to ease through the fence. Maybe this was the dance I knew best, this low, twisted stoop. Broken glass gave a shine to the ground, and rusted scrap lay everywhere.

At the yard beyond the last ruts of the road, I studied the ruin of the homestead, cataloged its pluck. The outhouse door was a self-closing marvel with polished pine handle, and syrup-can holder for toilet paper, the tin snipped neat, rolled, and finished smooth. In the house, the window glass was long gone, but a memory of pink paint lingered on the walls. From inside, the door framed a bare tree's reach. I sifted the debris on the floor, and there was a square of blue. After six years of winter and sun, there lay the book I had leafed through by evening light in 1982, then set down: *New Heavens and a New Earth*. The pages turned yellow from my fingers, a rasp of cheap paper made silky by dust. In the boldest print, I read "First Edition: TWO MILLION COPIES." I remembered that exuberant phrase. I was six years deeper into life, as I read from its words again:

> "Behold, I create new heavens and a new earth; and the former things shall not be remembered, nor come into mind."                                   Isaiah, 65:17

> God proceded to build the rib that he had taken from the man into a woman.

It was first when God's woman gave birth to the Kingdom
A.D. 1914 and God caught it up to his throne that God
planted or put the new heavens in power.

What has religion done for mankind?

Their life and activity will go on forever, far beyond the age
of any tree on earth.

I looked around at the walls of the hut, how they had been
pieced together like a quilt from the slim pine boards of fruit
boxes. It had taken four hundred boxes, by my count, to line
the four walls. I thought of my beads, how they might be
joined to make a whole thing. I thought of the hoard of small
sensations I had writ into the little notebook I carried, how
someday they might braid their way into a story to tell my
daughter or my friends. Out the shattered window, a mile
down the slope the city and the railyard seethed, where en-
gines rumbled and shot up smoke, and the long squeal of steel
on steel marked the coupling of a train. Out the doorway a
mound of coal dust hunched in the yard, and beyond it the
clutter of TV tubes were stacked awry, aerials, and cabinets,
where this homesteader's repair service must have stashed
them. I set the blue book down where the floor was littered,
and by old habit, in spite of Isaiah, I invited former things to
come to mind. I gathered them, because my new heaven
would have to come from the tatters of the old.

I thought of the meadowlark at the Heart of the Monster,
the ragged flag at the peak of Heart Mountain. I thought of
the white stone knife, the woman's name on a slip of paper in
the cedar grove. I thought of Thomas Shakespeare's grave at
St. Stephens, with its crimson cross and ring of stones. I
remembered Homer's cry in Jackson: "In just a little while, all
we have will be taken from us!" And Roe's whisper: "Will you
sing that story for us, please?"

Someone here had tried to homestead the waste land with
a cabin pieced from scrap, to hold true to a vision of the new

world, but to earn daily bread by repairing the TV sets of the old. This was the watchtower above the plain of common life. The wind must have torn their souls, and at the barbwire threshhold, where I had found relics from the wrestle of human love, they must have gritted their teeth and trod on foot toward the city at the end. I had driven west from that city with my family, and had come back alone. I stood beside the juniper tree that sweetened the place with resin. It twitched, and I did too. Evening stole toward the city below us, flowing down in one long sweep from Kingport Mountain.

# she Who Watches

MY JOURNEY WAS ENDING, and I fought its end. I didn't feel ready for the city yet. I didn't feel ready for home. At dusk, the car hummed and whistled, healed of its recent trouble, steady on. My bed lay rolled in the back, the sleeping bag my brother had given. In its flimsy cardboard case, I had the old nylon-string guitar my sister had loaned me for seven years. My clothes were stowed in a box. I planned to meet a friend at the Elks Club dance in Bozeman, if my car held out. So I was heading north and west at evening through sifting snow, at the south edge of Montana, down the long corridor of lodgepole pine when I saw deer on the road, first the emerald glints of their eyes, then the ghost shapes poised, and I jammed into a long skid, into the shriek of the tires and the skittish drift of the car toward the one, where the others scattered away but she did a slow pirouette, broadside gray where she turned in the headlights, hurtling toward me, throwing back her head when the grille tapped her rump just as the car slumped to a stop, and she bounded away. My heart pounded, and I smelled the burnt panic of the car. I looked up through the windshield. There were no clouds at all. Snow was falling from the stars.

Nightmares happen, sometimes turning in the last instant to the miracle collision of change.

The night led me forward, out from the forest, toward the gathering of lights in the valley. In Bozeman then, I walked the boisterous neon strip of Saturday night. There were so many lights they burned in the stream of cars, lurching and traveling by the red light halt, the green light parade between the rows of lit shop windows. I leaned on the shoulder of a parking meter felt the cold metal of its skin. Four women climbed laughing out of a truck. A passing car honked twice, the wolf whistle of the horn. The four turned inward for a few words, then laughed again and walked. I followed them for a few blocks, and turned in after them at the Elks Club door.

In the blue haze of the lounge fat with music, I scanned the crowd for my old friend and her new husband. I leaned on a wall that throbbed, and dancers worked the floor. In the glimmer of party light, I thought I saw her dancing, a fling on two feet against the strobe. The flat faces of the bands' guitars flashed their shine across the room, splashing the back wall with light. I watched the dancer. She was graceful, but she was someone else. I carried my glass of gold beer, searched the throng, and felt the music raise a buzz in my fingertips.

Then I was outside, walking. I zigzagged through the darker neighborhoods, threading the pooled shadow of plum trees and the bold arena of corner streetlights. Sometimes I could see the stars, or the lit glimmer of a curtained window. And then there they were, my friend and her man, turning toward me under a streetlight half a block away. When I saw him look at her, I felt a happy twinge. Before I heard a word, I heard her laugh, and I felt grateful for the way he made her happy. Sometimes it happens that way, too.

They put me up in the upstairs room they'd set aside for their first child, due soon, and I slept deeper than I had in days. Even when a neighbor dog woke me at midnight, I felt at rest. I remembered how her dogs had welcomed me, Thea wagging, Rose barking and scared.

"Rose!" my friend had said. "Shush!" She had turned to

me. "Someone must have beat her," she said, "before I got her." Rose backed away, with a last yelp. "Rose!" said my friend. "He's okay. Okay?"

In the night, I listened to each word of the dog, somewhere down the street. If lonely hearts could bark, the city would resound. My breath came slow. The leaves of the cottonwood tapped my window. The barking rested, then came in another tired frenzy. My life had pounded me. Some man beat Rose. The streetlight printed a thin curtain folded on the wall. I felt my mind come open fold by fold, and I slept.

In the morning we fed well, coffeed up, and each picked a bicycle from the flock in the yard. It was their Sunday custom to take the dogs and tour yard sales, and we made the rounds. Rain on the streets, sun in the sky, and we spun along the sidewalk for some blocks until we saw a red-lettered sign and swung aside. They shopped for more bicycles, God knows why. I bought a used Stetson because it was a bargain, though half a size too small. Maybe I could wear it in the rain, said my friend, stretch it out. I jammed it on my head, and we rode on. Downtown, on the impulse of the day, I bought a steel-string acoustic guitar on sale at Pete's Music Store. With the guitar in my arms, my fingers working the strings, I felt my life change from nylon to steel. Something just there, at the fretted neck of the song, felt right. I slung it over my shoulder, and we rode home. At the house, I wrapped the guitar in a blanket at the back of the car, shouted so long to my friends, and headed west.

Cruising at the maximum legal speed, as I went barreling down a freeway canyon with a convoy of trucks, a flock of tumbleweeds came billowing toward us in the wind. Some came single, some clenched in pairs, a big one ran alone with a covey following. The big one dashed into my grill, held there shuddering a moment, then bounced against the windshield and spun away. I drove wild against the wind, and through the orbit of long curves the car shook and caught hold, shaggy and happy in its old thousands of miles, spinning headlong forward.

My journey was ending. Coming around toward home, I yearned for temptation. Every small road begged me to turn aside, every track away over the fields. Every canyon urged a secret, every pine grove wished me to slow down easy, turn off, maybe get stuck and learn something. A dry wash glittered. Thickets of willow shook and asked me in. When I stopped for coffee, every cafe beauty spoke life with a glance. When a face seemed to question at the eyes, I was so gullible I believed what was never said. I carried it back to the car, told it to the windshield on the road again. And the world conspired with my whispered stories. Every handsome shack by the road, every barn told chapters. Shadows in cliffs spoke cave, sagewood fire at evening. Every lone house told me take another name, start over, be local here. I lived the native longing of tree, river, stone, barbwire line.

At the Montana restaurant called the Happy Bungalow, in Turah, neon by the door on the left burned the word "Lounge," and the door on the right blazed "Sizzling Steaks." I punched through the right-hand door, and went past the bar to a dim table at the back. The place was hopping with hungry travelers, and I felt private, overlooked in the din. I nibbled crackers. They had five kinds, a touch of generosity. Then I cleared my paper placemat and took out my pen to chart my journey. First I drew a long wandering line, with little circles at the knuckles of change, the places where I had learned. My line traveled like a river without clear benefit of gravity, kinking and doubling back on itself. Then my pen tried to go west from the Happy Bungalow, and stalled. An empty corner of the map would not fill in. Blank and small, it yearned. White, it blurred. It held my magnitude of sorrow.

Travel had given me sensation, a power of whim, deep meetings with friends and strangers. I looked up at the blue marlin mounted on the barroom wall. I watched the waitress stagger across the room with a huge platter of steak. The Happy Bungalow felt boisterous with simple hungers. The desert had fed me well. Certain places heal. I knew this on the road. But I didn't know what it would take to heal my life at home.

It would take the killing of something in me to go back at all.

And yet, the map on my placemat was dense with stories. I could read the line I had drawn like *quippu*, that knotted string of the Inca messengers their kings had coded with detail. The road for me had tangled in beautiful ways. I remembered a hemp cord I had seen in the museum at Lapwai, a cord some anonymous Nez Perce woman had knotted to recall the seasons of her life. Her life was short but the cord was long, the message of the knots secret and full. Her fingers could tell its stories blind. Maybe mine was more like kinked barbwire: terrible spikes on a steel twist. I remembered my confusion at the Arapaho graves. I remembered my stitch of longing in Jackson. But some of them were sweet. I remembered early evening on Polecat Bench, when a deer was crossing the canyon below me, and I sat down, took out my harmonica, began to play soft scales, a bluesy pleading. She stepped closer, turned her head, her ears swiveling, taking in the music, my strand of wind, then turned away but gently, stepped into the trees.

I had eight hanks of beads I had bought at Fort Hall. I had two-thousand miles of sensation pocketed in my soul. The map between my hands showed where I had jumped into the daylight, where I paid life tuition, where I held amulets from the shrines of this land and my people. Along my pilgrim way, I remembered older forms of coherence than my culture taught me. There was a time when places were named by something that happened there. I was learning my territory by the old ways, and I named places by the stories they gave me:

Woman's Name where Elk Lick Salt
Coyote Bends the Wire
Sleep Cold in the Stones
Kin of the Wetback
Long Maned Woman on a Running Horse
Taxes in the Laundromat
Hat too Small

I folded my map when the waitress came to me with a glass of water and a grin, and I ordered the biggest steak they had. I thought of myself as a vegetarian, but not in Montana. Not Wyoming, either. Not Idaho. I felt like a bear there, a clumsy one, raw from the cave. While I waited for my steak, I tuned in to eavesdrop from the booths behind me. There was a different style of story at each station. Some gruff voice was telling a betrayal.

"So he gets on the phone to her, says, 'Hello, Dora? This was your husband Jake.' 'Was?' she says. 'I'm leaving,' he says. And that was that."

"That's mean," said a softer voice. "Why did he even bother to call?"

There was a splintering of glass from the kitchen, and a shout. The waitress, cruising across the room with a crushing load, turned a moment, then carried forward and brought her tray to a landing with a groan. Then she smiled, and started handing around relish trays. The kitchen ruckus died, and I turned my head and tuned to another conversation, where two couples had just recognized each other in the dim light. I couldn't see them, but they were close behind me, and I had a clear connection.

"Bob, Doris, is that you?" said a husky voice.

"Hey, Carl, Mona. What you two been doing?"

"Living the good life, Bob."

"What's the good life?"

"Killing fish and hunting mushroom, mostly."

"Mushroom?"

"Morels."

Then the steaks started coming, and they all got busy. Mine arrived, sputtering on the platter the waitress clunked down before me.

"A-1?" she said.

"Worcestershire," I said. She brought it, and left me be. I sawed off a thick bite, and lived awhile like a predator. As I chewed, I unfolded my AAA highway map of the west. Every state was a different color, but the roads were red, and they held it all together. I turned from the map to my steaming plate. The steak itself had bumps and ridges and little valleys of fat. I worked that landscape with my knife and fork. And I read the road the map showed west from the Happy Bungalow. My three-day stall for car repair in Pocatello had exempted me from the Coeur d'Alene conference, and I read the highways, and tasted the sweet pang of salt on my meat, and suddenly the restaurant was gone, my hands were at the wheel, and I had turned south from Missoula for the Lochsa road again. My teeth ached, my eyes burned. The meal had filled me, but something deep was going away. My journey was receding behind me. West at Lolo, up over the summit, I drove down the long run of the Lochsa River. I was hurtling. Evening light settled against tree and stone, every bluff rising where the river turned, every glitter of water where the rapids stepped down. The land did things well. Rock made sense. Water traveled exactly, celebrating the purpose of gravity in fine detail. Pine had a logic: root down, green up, and hold. I followed the road.

The land lay dark as I swept west through Lewiston, and up over the wheat hills, through Pomeroy, Dixie, Walla Walla, Wallula, Umatilla. The road's rhythm, and starlight, calmed me. I felt myself of a size with what was coming. I didn't know what that might be, but I would.

I watched tail-light, headlight, reflection, and the dull ribbon of highway furling under in a blur. It had been night so long, I couldn't guess the end. I'd forgotten to wind my watch, and time stretched whole, night seamless. At the bridge north from The Dalles, I turned to cross the Columbia, having one more visit to pay before I went home. I had to stand by She Who Watches. I knew where she would be.

The park at Horse Thief Reservoir had closed at dusk. I read the sign in my lights, but from the highway I could see the ranger was asleep. I was a pilgrim, would hurt nothing. I left the car and walked past his house, down toward the darkness of the Columbia, where it carried the flat veil of reflected lights from the Oregon side, moved them west.

My feet found the sharp gravel embedded in tar. Sensation swept me up. Or fear swept me up, sharpening each sensation. Maybe life tuition was not a payment but a food. Maybe the places had nourished me until I was another man. I wouldn't know, until I got home, and hard things happened. I was a-fraid. I had to find She Who Watches, and touch the river.

I remembered how the road turns halfway down. By star-light, the deepest darkness turned, and I followed it. Sage and grass rustled pale along the edges. Then came the end of pavement, and I walked a gravel rut. Then the twin gleam of the railroad tracks beckoned, and I turned west to follow them. Each tie cast a softer glimmer my step found. She Who Watches, the petroglyph stone face somewhere above the track, would be there. I had to sit by her, before I pulled snug the drawstring on this two- thousand miles, this two weeks of wandering. I was cold, and knotted my fists.

The dark held something for me. I stopped on the track where I thought she might be. The river, I could hear it now, sipping at the reeds and stones below me, in its deep surge west. I put that sound at my back. I wanted to find the stone face with my fingers. I stumbled off the raised causeway of the track, and touched stone all along the cliff: warm, smooth at the fracture lines that make basalt honest and plain. The facets of the cliff addressed me dimly. Where was she? I crouched, and waited. Somewhere, a bird on the water skit-tered away. My stillness must have frightened it. Coot, maybe. Over my shoulder, I could see how stars settled on the river, their sweep. Maybe this was the Paiute second night, the deeper one at the heart of the whole dark.

From the east, I felt the tremor of a train, then heard it, a grounded tone in the stone notch where I leaned. It grew louder, came on, grumbled in the rock, then flashed into view around the bend. The train's roving eye came spindling along the track, breathing toward me. Maybe my eyes glittered in that light, and the engineer saw me as I had seen the deer, where I stood up, and turned at the foot of the embankment. The headlamp burned a spiral as it came. I faced the cliff, and stared. There she was, She Who Watches. She took my breath: her square bear ears, her concentric eyes, the small box mouth not ten feet from me. In the flickering thunder of the trainlight, I moved to sit below her, to put my ear against her mouth. And the train clapped thunder, passing at my back. I listened to that pounding in the stone, until the train went away west, dwindled into silence, and the river murmured again.

As I pressed my ear against stone, I remembered how Coyote said to her, *You, woman, you, Tsagaglalal, you go up on the cliff and watch over the people. You look down, be still, wait.* And there she has been, though the dam went in, though the people were driven from their village, though water covered their home. I turned. On the river, into the stars, I saw what she saw. The world was dark, but alive. Centuries passed. Sage yet breathed. Stone held still, but sometimes snapped, clattered from itself in little pieces. If stone could, I could. Cold shook me. The deep night hugged me. I felt it happening, the little splintering of change. Cold was not the root of my shivering.

Along the thread of road on the Oregon side, I saw long trucks with their display of running lights carrying neat little cities toward the east, the west. And beyond the highway, I saw the hump of cliff that rose from the river there, the dim palisade of volcanic stone. I saw a scatter of streetlights glimmer in that village they call The Dalles, the narrows, way over there in Oregon, in the world where I had started.

The stars felt close. I leaned back against my stone. I had driven so far, there was no hurry now. I had risked my life, for certain places heal. I had traveled to them. I had listened, watched, had slept on the earth. I had learned the magnitude of my sorrow, sketched it on a placemat. I didn't need to be happy, to savor some predicted calm. I needed to broaden my definition of satisfaction. Let it be pitch, stone, silence, and the varieties of clumsy change. It would be enough if I could be honest about my confusion, and go on.

The stars flung outward from where I crouched. My sense

of home had to open like that. My land was wide, and on it, I could live. I stood up toward the stars.

But I had a rock in my shoe, and as I loosed the lace and fished it out, hunched over, balanced in the dark, I knew. I crossed the tracks, felt my slow way down the boulder riprap, to the river. On a stone at the water's edge, I shook off both shoes. I unbuttoned my shirt, careful so the notebook and pen would hold to their pocket. I took off my socks, then my trousers with their pocketed knife and watch. I hung the beaded bag from my neck over a dim twig of willow, and slipped with a gasp into the water, raising a line of cold around me like a hem, then buoyant at the ribs and shoulders where I entered the river, deeper than me, carrying me when my feet skidded off the last stone. Delight or cold shivered a deep shout out of me, and I churned and rolled, some new animal, throwing back my head to whimper, gasp, laugh. Lochsa Road threaded through the stars. I rolled again and faced east, paddled steadily to stay in place. Now, at this place, the pil-grim road had brought me home. Home was the size of my skin, of the West, of starlight and daylight and dark. I wore the river thin and ancient at my lips.

# BIOGRAPHICAL NOTES

*Kim R. Stafford* grew up in Oregon, Iowa, Indiana, California, and Alaska, where he followed his parents as they taught and traveled through the west. He has taught at Lewis & Clark College since 1979, where he directs the Northwest Writing Institute, and teaches courses in ethnographic and environmental writing, and in lyrical prose.

He has received creative writing fellowships from the National Endowment for the Arts; and his book *Having Everything Right* won a Western States Book Awards Citation for Excellence in 1986. He holds a Ph.D. in medieval literature from the University of Oregon, and lives in Portland with his daughter, Rosemary.


*Hannah Hinchman* is an artist and writer living in Jackson Hole, Wyoming. She is the author of *A Life in Hand: Creating the Illuminated Journal*, (1991). Watercolor is her current preferred medium; the drawings in this book are done with a tiny brush and india ink.

Illustrations by Hannah Hinchman
Book design and production by
Tanya Gonzales and Andrew Caldwell
Production assistance by
Penny Bosshardt and Judi Lanphier
The type is Goudy with Goudy display
Printed by McNaughton & Gunn
on acid-free paper